FOOTBALL SHORTS

1,001 OF THE GAME'S FUNNIEST ONE-LINERS

GLENN LIEBMAN

CB
CONTEMPORARY BOOKS

Library of Congress Cataloging-in-Publication Data

Liebman, Glenn.
    Football shorts : 1,001 of the game's funniest one-liners / Glenn
  Liebman.
        p.   cm.
      ISBN 0-8092-3215-4
      1. Football—United States—Humor.   2. Football—United States—
  Quotations, maxims, etc.   I. Title.
  GV950.5.L54   1997
  796.332'02'07—dc21   97-26159
                                                                   CIP

Published by Contemporary Books
An imprint of NTC/Contemporary Publishing Company
4255 West Touhy Avenue, Lincolnwood (Chicago), Illinois 60646-1975 U.S.A.
Copyright © 1997 by Glenn Liebman
All rights reserved. No part of this book may be reproduced, stored in a
retrieval system, or transmitted in any form or by any means, electronic,
mechanical, photocopying, recording, or otherwise, without the prior
permission of NTC/Contemporary Publishing Company.
Manufactured in the United States of America
International Standard Book Number: 0-8092-3215-4

17   16   15   14   13   12   11   10   9   8   7   6   5   4   3   2   1

To my father, Bernie,
who taught me to persevere
and to never let anyone dissuade you
from following your dreams.

ACKNOWLEDGMENTS

As always, I'd like to thank my agent, Philip Spitzer, and Nancy Crossman, the visionary behind this series of books. I'd also like to thank my editor, Alina Cowden, for her patience, good humor, and knowledge. I'd also like to thank my project editor, Craig Bolt, who has provided valuable technical assistance, dedication, and friendship.

I'd like to especially thank all of football's funnymen: Bum Phillips, Lou Holtz, Bobby Bowden, Alex Karras, John Madden, John McKay, and so many more. I'd like to also thank the Jets of the late 1960s for making me a lifelong football fan.

My mother, Frieda, deserves special praise. Probably the best Liebman family story is the one about how she was once mistaken for Joe Namath's mother. It is a long story, but she handled the whole episode with her usual wonderful sense of humor. Thirty years later, the story still makes me laugh; it is emblematic of the kind of good-humored and cheerful person my mother was.

I'd also like to thank my brother, Bennett, for making me into a football fan by letting me go to Jets games with his cool group of friends thirty years ago.

My little pal Frankie deserves recognition for his help on this book. His constant good humor reminds me how lucky I am to be his dad. Though he currently is the world's biggest basketball fanatic, it won't be too long before football becomes a major part of his life.

Finally, as always, the person most responsible for all the good things is my wife, Kathy. She continues to provide me with inspiration, friendship, and humor. She will always be the best thing that ever happened to me.

INTRODUCTION

I must love to suffer. That is the only way to explain my lifelong love affair with the Jets.

It started when I was a kid growing up in Long Island. The Jets used to have their preseason practices ten minutes from my house. My friends and I would ride our bikes over there to watch their workouts. We dreamed of getting Joe Namath's autograph. That never happened, but we did get to meet lots of players from the Jets' glory years.

I still proudly display my Matt Snell, Emerson Boozer, and Ed "The Flea" Bell autographs almost thirty years later. That attachment and loyalty to the Jets remain today largely because of those great memories.

Now I live in Albany, New York, which is ten minutes from where the Giants practice. My hope is that one day my two-and-a-half-year-old son will have acquired similar fond memories and will become a lifelong Giants fan. (Why should he suffer like I have?)

The one thing the current Jets conjure up is humor. Anyone who sat through last year's 1–15 season has to have a good sense of humor. Thankfully, there are a lot of football players and coaches who also display a great sense of humor.

When it comes to naming the funniest figures in sports, I tend to favor the characters from the book I'm working on at the time. When I put together *Baseball Shorts*, I thought Casey Stengel was the funniest sports figure in history. With *Golf Shorts*, I thought it was Lee Trevino. With *Basketball Shorts*, it was Frank Layden. Now I am convinced that it's Bum Phillips.

Here are a few Bumisms to whet your appetite: On passing his physical exam, Phillips commented, "If I drop dead tomorrow, at least I know I died in good health." Asked if he played college football, he replied, "I thought I did until I looked at old game films."

With the likes of Bum, Lou Holtz (on his Arkansas team being pelted with oranges at the Orange Bowl: "I'm glad we're not going to the Gator Bowl"), John McKay (on the fan mail he received as the Tampa Bay Buccaneers coach: "It was about three-to-one that I was not an SOB. But there were a lot of ones."), Alex Karras (on his college career at the University of Iowa: "I was only there for two terms—Truman's and Eisenhower's"), and so many more, this is a book that will keep you laughing from spring practice through the Super Bowl.

"I never threw in the off-season. I've been around so long, I could be blindfolded and spun around a dozen times and I'd still know where the goalposts are."

George Blanda

"The thing is that by the time I finished playing, I was too old to be starting out as a coach."

*George Blanda, on playing in
four decades*

"When you win, you're an old pro. When you lose, you're an old man."

Charlie Conerly

"Elvin is so old, he had to use a jumper cable to get started last year."

*Doug Dieken, on 14-year veteran
Elvin Bethea*

"Every time I see my name in the paper, it says Roy Green, 34. I'm starting to think my last name is 34."

Roy Green

"After 12 years, the old butterflies come back. Well, I guess at my age you can call them moths."

> *Franco Harris, on playing for the Seahawks after 12 seasons with the Steelers*

"He may be the only kicker to kick and collect social security at the same time."

> *John McKay, on 41-year-old Jan Stenerud*

"The only time age will ever hurt a team is when all the old players quit at the same time."

> *Jack Pardee*

"The last time he leaned over to take the snap, he couldn't come out of the crouch."

> *Don Rickles, on George Blanda*

"Formaldehyde."

> *John Riggins, when asked to what he attributed his long playing career*

"Contrary to public opinion, I have not worn that uniform before."

Jackie Slater, at age 40, on wearing a nostalgic Rams uniform from 1951

"I may go on forever, because statistics say that few men die at the age of 100."

Amos Alonzo Stagg, on turning 100

"When you get old, everything is hurting. When I get up in the morning, it sounds like I'm making popcorn."

Lawrence Taylor, on turning 33

ACTING

"I can get to the bathroom on Monday morning without crawling."

Lyle Alzado, on how acting differs from football

"I like theater crowds a lot better. They don't scream or drink beer or throw snowballs. They might all fall asleep, but they don't boo, and most of all they don't do the wave."

Dean Biasucci, kicker and actor, on the difference between movie crowds and football crowds

"Impersonating a football coach—that's all I've ever done."

Bobby Bowden, on playing a football coach on the TV show Evening Shade

"It's hard to tell what kind of actress she was. All I ever saw her in were Abbott and Costello movies. Let's just say she's a great mom."

Mark Harmon, college football star and actor, on his mom Elyse Knox

"I only want to be in the kill movies. It ain't no fun unless you get to kill somebody. I don't want to be in *Love Story*."

Lawrence Taylor, on pursuing an acting career

4

"I was doing a facial survey on behalf of a league-wide poll I'm taking. I know Steve is a Gillette Atra blade man."

> *Lester Hayes, on holding receiver*
> *Steve Watson's face in the mud during*
> *a game*

"First you want to make the team. Then you want to be an All-Pro. Then you want to be in the Hall of Fame. But before that, you want to do a Lite beer commercial."

> *Charlie Waters*

ADVICE AND CONSENT

"My athletes are always willing to accept my advice as long as it doesn't conflict with their views."

> *Lou Holtz*

AGENTS

"It was a rash statement, and I'd like to apologize to every vulture in the sky."

Mike Gottfried, former University of Pittsburgh coach, on his statement that all sports agents are vultures

ALKA—SELTZER

"I can't believe these salaries. All we needed in the old days was enough dough to buy a hunk of kosher salami, a loaf of Jewish rye, and a case of Schlitz."

Art Donovan, on current football salaries

ALL—AMERICAN

"My definition of an All-American is a player who has weak opposition and a poet in the press box."

Bob Zuppke, former University of Illinois coach

"I don't say George Allen is conservative, but running our offense is like driving a car in second gear."

Sonny Jurgensen

"He's great to the old guys. He's got one trainer just to treat varicose veins."

Alex Karras

"I think the ultimate win for George would have been 2–0."

Joe Theismann, on Allen's love of defense

"I once gave George a five-year-old dog and he swapped it for two ten-year-old kittens."

Edward Bennett Williams, on Allen's propensity for acquiring veterans

"We gave him an unlimited expense account and he's already exceeded it."

Edward Bennett Williams, Redskins owner

MARCUS ALLEN

"He carries so many tacklers with him, he's listed in the Yellow Pages under Public Transportation."
Bob Hope, on Marcus Allen

ALOHA

"That's a tough walk from here."
Lee Corso, former India University coach, on Mike Ocasek, a walk-on from Hawaii

"It's very difficult to drive a pickup truck from Lubbock to Hawaii."
Hayden Fry, Iowa coach, on Alamo Bowl opponent Texas Tech, who wanted to play in the Aloha Bowl

"Cattle have no alumni."

> *Sammy Baugh, on why he retired to raise cattle*

"After losing to Florida the way we did last year, it might not be a good idea for me to get out on a boat with some of our alumni."

> *Bobby Bowden, on agreeing to go golfing with alumni, but not fishing*

"I'm not going to wear this for at least 24 hours. After 2–9 and 1–10 seasons, I'm a little edgy about anything that ticks."

> *Lee Corso, on getting a watch as a gift from alumni*

"I always preferred a running offense, but I was smart enough to put in one long incomplete pass per quarter just for the alumni."

> *Duffy Daugherty*

"They end every season with a 'but.' Like, 'We had a good season, but. . . .' "

*Lou Holtz, on what alumni have
in common*

"I ask them to give us a lot of money, but not their two cents."

Joe Paterno, on alumni boosters

"They were all home games and I never had to worry about the alumni."

*Homer Rice, Georgia Tech athletic
director, on why being the coach of a
prison team was his best job*

"A good season for the alumni is when the team goes 11–0 and the coach gets fired."

Pepper Rodgers

"My biggest problems are defensive linemen and offensive alumni."

Bo Schembechler

ARENA FOOTBALL

"Maybe this means we'll get an arena
football team."

> *Rick Leach, Blue Jays player, on*
> *the Blue Jays losing to the*
> *Yankees 15–14*

ARMY—NAVY

"If it was, Army and Navy would be playing for the
national championship every year."

> *Bobby Bowden, asked if discipline*
> *was the key to winning*

ASSISTANT COACHES

"I don't hire anybody not brighter than I am. If
they're not brighter than I am, I don't need them."

> *Bear Bryant*

"I once looked up at the ceiling and saw a spider doing a bench press."

> *Joe Gibbs, on the motivational strength of Redskins weight-lifting coach Dan Riley*

"If you want to drop off the face of the earth, just be an assistant coach."

> *Bob Griese*

"There's a quote in the Bible that says, 'Joseph died leaning on his staff.' The same thing will be said about me when I pass away."

> *Lou Holtz*

ASTRODOME

"If it's the Eighth Wonder of the World, the rent is the ninth."

> *Bud Adams, Oilers owner, on the Astrodome*

ATHLETIC DIRECTORS

"No athletic director holds office longer than two losing football coaches in a row."
Duffy Daugherty

"I just found out what 'emeritus' means. It means working without pay."
Moose Krause, former Notre Dame athletic director, on his new emeritus title

ATTENDANCE

"This place was so empty, they could have held archery practice."
Bill Parcells, on a poorly attended preseason game

BABY TALK

"The scouts are waiting for the offspring of that matchup."

> *Dick Enberg, on the marriage of*
> *former Jets guard Chris Ward to*
> *Jim Brown's daughter*

"Like a baby—for two and a half hours."

> *Bum Phillips, asked how he slept*
> *after a loss*

"We've got so many kids on our roster, we're going to be the first team in football history with an equipment order for Pampers."

> *Ray Sewalt, TCU recruiter, on a*
> *young team*

BAMBI

"If Lance had played the piano, he would have probably sounded like Arthur Rubenstein."

> *Sid Gillman, on all-time great*
> *Lance Alworth*

" 'Bout all I did was stick with it."

> *Bear Bryant, on winning his 315th*
> *game, passing Amos Alonzo Stagg*
> *to become football's all-time*
> *winningest coach*

"The last time I received anything from the NCAA, it was probation."

> *Bear Bryant, on receiving an*
> *award from the NCAA after*
> *becoming the winningest coach*
> *in college football history*

"The definition of an atheist in Alabama is a person who doesn't believe in Bear Bryant."

> *Wally Butts, University of Georgia*
> *athletic director*

"The Bear can take his and beat yours and take yours and beat his."

> *Jake Gaither, former Florida*
> *A & M coach*

"If he can't do it, then he sure knows where the stumps are buried."

> *Ara Parseghian, asked if Bear Bryant could walk on water*

"I saw the Bear play the Bear."

> *Bum Phillips, when asked if he had any interest in seeing Gary Busey play Bryant in a movie*

"He won because he coached people, not football."

> *Bum Phillips*

BEARS

"Don't ask me to name names, because anyone I leave out will be gnawing at my ankles in the pileup."

> *Pete Brock, Patriots offensive lineman, on the dominant Bears defensive unit of 1985–86*

"I always enjoy animal acts."

President Calvin Coolidge, when
asked if he wanted to meet several
members of the Chicago Bears,
in 1925

"Some teams are fair-haired. We're not. Some teams are the Smiths—we're the Grabowskis."

Mike Ditka

"The only ball I ever got in Chicago, I stole."

Charlie Ford, former Bears
cornerback, on receiving a game
ball after being traded

"I really just have to see a picture of the Chicago Bears once a week and I don't miss anything."

Archie Manning, when asked if he
missed football

"The Bears aren't very genteel. Some teams tend to remove the football from you. The Bears remove you from the football. It's quicker."

Jim Murray, on the 1986 Bears

"The game would be in progress and this hot dog vendor would be walking out there in front of our bench, leaning over our players to make a sale to the fans."

Tex Schramm, on George Halas's strategy of selling chairs at Wrigley Field near the opponents' bench

"None of the Bears can read, so it won't make a difference."

Keith Van Horne, on a number of Bears players writing books critical of each other

"They're so tough that when they finish sacking the quarterback, they go after his family in the stands."

Tim Wrightman, on the Bears defense of the mid-'80s

BENGALS

"The thought of standing out there without sweatshirts on was horrible. But we decided that the Chargers play in perpetual springtime; we might really do a number on their heads."

> *Dave Lapham, Bengals offensive lineman, on playing against the Chargers in a playoff game in short sleeves, despite below-zero temperatures*

BEVERAGE OF CHOICE

"Cold."

> *Bruce Collie, 49ers lineman, on his favorite kind of beer*

"We didn't have anything like steroids. If I wanted to get pumped up, I drank a case of beer."
> *Art Donovan*

"They won't let me have a beer. The last time I went this long without one was either the two weeks before I was born or the two weeks after. I can't remember."

> *Jim McMahon, on sustaining an injury that forced him to go into the hospital for several days*

"Drink the first. Sip the second slowly. Skip the third."

> *Knute Rockne, advice to players on drinking beer*

BILINGUAL

"I'm going to study Spanish so I can use a few expletives in my press conferences next season."

> *Francis Peay, former Northwestern coach, on why he was taking a class in Spanish during the off-season*

BILLS

"It's too soon after the car wreck to say we're feeling better."

> *Marv Levy, meeting with his team after its fourth Super Bowl loss in a row*

"This is like Dracula. You've got to put a stake in their heart, and then you still wonder if it's in there."

> *Bill Parcells, on the Patriots defeating the Bills and ensuring they would not make their fifth Super Bowl appearance in a row*

"You know it was bad when the only person taking pictures in the locker room was my dad."

> *Fred Smerlas, on the bad days in Buffalo*

BLUE DEVILS

"As the team progresses, we'll be a progression team."

Steve Sloan, Duke coach, on prospects for the coming year

BO KNOWS

"It might turn from hobby to hobble."

Gene Mauch, on Bo Jackson deciding to take up football as a hobby

BODY PARTS

"A football player is like a prostitute—your body is only worth something for so long. When it's no good anymore, nobody wants it."

Larry Grantham

BOILERMAKERS

"I look better in black than I do in orange."

Diane Akers, on the advantages of her husband, Fred Akers, being fired by Texas and hired by Purdue

BOOK BEAT

"Ransom notes."

Alex Karras, on being asked to name the most profitable type of writing

"They write more books."

Darrell Royal, on how players of today are different than those from the old days

"But the real tragedy was that 15 hadn't been colored yet."

Steve Spurrier, Florida coach, telling fans that a fire at the Auburn football dorm had destroyed 20 books

BOOTS ARE MADE
FOR WALKING

"They don't have enough cows up in Michigan to make his boots."

> *Bum Phillips, on why 6'7",*
> *350-pound Angelo Fields, from the*
> *University of Michigan, didn't wear*
> *cowboy boots*

BOWL GAMES

"The Rose Bowl is the only bowl I've ever seen that I didn't have to clean."

> *Erma Bombeck*

"I'm glad we're not going to the Gator Bowl."

> *Lou Holtz, on being pelted with*
> *oranges when Arkansas was in the*
> *Orange Bowl*

"You can bet their float will reach the judges' stand by January 6."

> *Bob Hope, on the U.S. Postal Service*
> *having a float at the January 1 Rose*
> *Bowl Parade*

"In 1983, we got official Holiday Bowl watches. This year, they told us if we came back they'll fix our official Holiday Bowl watches."

> *Glen Kozlowski, on Brigham Young*
> *returning to the Holiday Bowl*
> *in 1984*

"Bowl games are not fun unless you win."

> *Darrell Royal*

BOWLING

"They don't like my overhand delivery."

> *Bubba Smith, on being barred from*
> *bowling alleys*

THE BOZ

"It's a good thing Brian was a third child, or he would have been the only one."

Kathy Bosworth, on her son

"In the long run, the cream always rises and the crap always sinks. And that's where he's gone—to the bottom."

John Elway, on Brian Bosworth

BRONCOS

"I won't say how tough our fans were, but I did my best broken-field running to my car after the game."

Floyd Little, after a bad season by the Broncos

"Orange Crush is soda water, baby. You drink it. It don't win football games."

Harvey Martin, after the Cowboys beat the Broncos—nicknamed the Orange Crush—in the '80 Super Bowl

"I left because of illness and fatigue. The fans were sick and tired of me."

John Ralston, on why he left as
Broncos coach

JIM BROWN

"When you've got a cannon, you fire it."

Paul Brown, asked if he used Jim
Brown too much

"Every time I tackle Jim Brown, I hear a dice game going on in my mouth."

Don Burroughs

"It's like tackling a locomotive."

Glenn Holtzman, on Jim Brown

"Give each guy on the line an ax."

Alex Karras, on the best way to stop
Jim Brown

"He's even better than I thought he was, and I thought he was the best."
Gino Marchetti

"Jimmy Brown was the finest all-around athlete I ever saw—he was a jock-of-all-trades."
Jon Weber

BROWNS

"There is absolutely no truth to the rumor that the Browns highlight film will be a Polaroid shot."
Art Modell, after a 5–11 season

"It's like having heart attacks. You can survive them, but there's always scar tissue."
Sam Rutigliano, Browns coach, on several last-minute defeats in 1978

"In those days, it was BYOB—Bring Your
Own Blocker."

> *Ricky Bell, on the early years of*
> *the Buccaneers*

"You do a lot of praying, but most of the time the
answer is 'no.'"

> *John McKay, on why coaching*
> *an expansion team is a*
> *religious experience*

"Every time I look up, it seems we're punting."

> *John McKay, on the early years of*
> *Tampa Bay*

"I think it's a good idea."

> *John Mckay, on the*
> *Buccaneers' execution*

"Sometimes I feel like I'm on the aft deck of the
Lusitania."

> *Bob Moore, Buccaneers tight end, on*
> *losing every game*

"I was going to get married after we won our first game. But we decided against it."

Dewey Selmon, on getting married during the Buccaneers' 26-game losing streak

"I don't have to go to the drive-in windows at McDonald's anymore."

Lee Roy Selmon, on the improving Buccaneers

"Dim."

Pat Toomay, on his memories from Tampa Bay's 0–14 season

"We're the only team in the history of the league that has a quarterback-coach controversy."

Sam Wyche, on Buccaneers quarterback coach Turk Schonert's interest in playing quarterback in an emergency

BUCKEYES

"My golf game reminds me of Woody Hayes's football game—three yards and a cloud of dust."
Bill Dooley, Wake Forest
football coach

DICK BUTKUS

"I wouldn't ever set out to hurt anybody deliberately unless it was important, like a league game or something."
Dick Butkus

"Whenever they gave him the game ball, he ate it."
Alex Hawkins, on Butkus

"One time he bit me. Another time he tried to break my ankle. Another time he grabbed my leg and tried to crack it over my knee. Nothing happened. I guess maybe my leg was too green."
MacArthur Lane, on Butkus

"He was like Moby Dick in a goldfish bowl."

*Steve Sabol, producer of NFL Films,
on the greatness of Butkus*

CALIFORNIA, HERE WE COME

"It wasn't luck. We practiced double-teaming the trombone player all week long."

*Joe Kapp, University of California
coach, on the famous last-second
play against Stanford, when the
Cal ball carrier ran through the
Stanford marching band to score
the winning touchdown*

EARL CAMPBELL

"It's like standing blindfolded in the middle of Interstate 75, dodging the cars and trying to tackle the biggest truck out there."

*Gary Burley, on trying to tackle
Earl Campbell*

"Bum's a great coach. He has a play for every situation—a handoff to Earl Campbell."

> *Bob Hope, on the genius of Bum*
> *Phillips as a coach*

"He ought to run for president, because if he runs for mayor, he'll beat me."

> *Jim McConn, Houston mayor, on the*
> *popularity of Earl Campbell*

"Comforting."

> *Dan Pastorini, on what it's like to*
> *hand off the ball to Campbell*

"Earl may not be in a class by himself, but whatever class he's in, it doesn't take long to call the roll."

> *Bum Phillips*

"When you tackle Campbell, it reduces your IQ."

> *Pete Wysocki*

CANADIAN
FOOTBALL LEAGUE

"I've been fined by the league so much I have no salary."

> *Ron Meyer, on the poor officiating in the CFL*

"We should be like brother to brother. Instead, we're more like cousins."

> *Mario Perry, on the lack of closeness of his Shreveport Pirates teammates*

CARDINAL (STANFORD)

"To beat a bunch of yuppies in uniform feels good."

> *Charles Burnham, San Jose State linebacker, on beating Stanford*

"It was the ugliest event at Busch Stadium since the tractor pull."

> *Roy Green, Cardinals receiver, on an*
> *awful game against the Eagles*

"Life goes on. I have it on good authority that babies were still born in Baltimore after the Colts pulled out."

> *Vincent Schoemehl, Jr., St. Louis*
> *mayor, on the Cardinals leaving*
> *St. Louis*

CENTER OF ATTENTION

"We're the only family I know of that plays catch without facing each other."

> *Jay Hilgenberg, NFL center, whose*
> *brother, Joel, was an NFL center,*
> *and whose dad and uncle were*
> *centers*

"If Steve Young's hands are worth $40 million, I wonder how much my rear end would go for."
Trevor Matick, on being Steve Young's center at BYU

CHARACTER

"The real make of a man is how he treats people who can never do anything for him."
Darrell Royal

CHEATING

"I told the administration I'd win the Big Ten championship in two years if they'd let me do two things—spend all the money I wanted to and cheat."
Lee Corso, on Indiana University

"If you cheat on the practice field, you'll cheat in the game. And if you cheat in the game, you'll cheat the rest of your life."
Vince Lombardi

CHEERLEADERS

"They're the girl-next-door types, if you happen to live next door to Caesar's Palace."

Bob Costas, on the Cincinnati Bengals' cheerleaders

CHICKEN LITTLE

"I no longer sleep. I roost."

Lee Corso, on all the chicken dinners he's been to as Indiana coach

CLOTHES MAKE THE MAN

"When you're this size, you don't have sizes—all you have is Xs. . . . Right now I'm between 3X and 4X."

Nate Newton, on the clothes he wears as a 325-pounder

"When I was young, I wanted to be the best coach in the world. Later, I just wanted to be the oldest."
John Bridgers, Florida State athletic director, on his days as a coach

"Sure I would. I'd miss him too."
Frank Broyles, Arkansas athletic director, asked if he would like coach Ken Hatfield as much if Arkansas lost half of its games

"I never thought college football would become like Central America. Kids don't understand it's supposed to be a dictatorship."
Beano Cook, on the lack of respect modern-day athletes give to coaches

"Some were defensive-minded, some offensive-minded, and some no-minded."
Boomer Esiason, on the six coaches he played for in six years

"If you're a pro coach, NFL stands for 'Not For Long.'"

Jerry Glanville

"A good coach needs three things: a patient wife, a loyal dog, and a great quarterback—not necessarily in that order."

Bud Grant

"One day you are drinking the wine, and the next day you are picking the grapes."

Lou Holtz, on the vagaries of coaching in the NFL

"Somebody said to me, 'How can you call the plays from the sideline when you can't see anything?' and I said, 'Well, that's the only place I ever watched a game from when I was playing.'"

Lou Holtz

"Absolutely. There are a thousand better coaches in the cities, but I'm the best in the country."

Lou Holtz, on the claim made by some that he's the best coach in the country

39

"Coaches who can outline plays are a dime a dozen. The ones who win get inside their players and motivate them."

Vince Lombardi

"Coaches have to watch for what they don't want to see and to listen to what they don't want to hear."

John Madden

"A genius in the NFL is a guy who won last week."

John McKay

"Coaching is like a bath—if you stay in long enough, it's not so hot."

Biggie Munn, Michigan State
athletic director

"It ruined my bologna sandwich [first game] and then I got sick again [second game]."

Don Nehlen, West Virginia coach,
during an off-week in which he
watched his team's next opponent,
Syracuse, win by 22 and then
watched Miami, their opponent in
two weeks, beat Penn State

"It feels very temporary."

Darrell Royal, asked how he felt
being named Coach of the Year

"A coach isn't as smart as they say he is when he wins, or as stupid when he loses."

Darrell Royal

"I have absolutely no problem with getting ahead and staying ahead."

Gene Stallings, describing his
coaching strategy

"When I got into the coaching business, I knew I was getting into a high-risk, high-profile profession, so I adopted a philosophy I've never wavered from. Yesterday is a canceled check, today is cash on the line, tomorrow is a promissory note."

Hank Stram

COAL MINER'S SONS

"Football is a game designed to keep coal miners off the streets."

Jimmy Breslin

COLLEGE DAYS

"I got a B.S. in B.S."

Bubba Baker, on his major in college

"It's kind of hard to rally around a math class."

Bear Bryant, on the role football plays in college life

"Academic survival."

Glenn Cameron, Bengals linebacker, on his major in college

"He got tired of his dad writing him for money."

Beano Cook, on why a basketball player dropped out of college

"Next thing you know, they'll be asking for soap."
Gary Fallon, Washington and Lee
coach, on players complaining about
no hot water in their dorm

"This job is better than I could get if I used my college degree, which at this point, I can't remember what it was in."
Bob Golic, on his two-year,
$1.5-million contract

"I never graduated from the University of Iowa, but I was only there for two terms—Truman's and Eisenhower's."
Alex Karras

"I won't get a football field named after me. Then again, I won't have to pay any alumni dues."
David Krieg, on his alma mater,
Milton College, closing down

"I thought I did until I looked at old game films."
Bum Phillips, asked if he played
college football

"When the pros talk a boy out of his degree to play for money, it's like talking against motherhood."

> *Darrell Royal, on George Sauer not staying for his redshirt year at Texas in the mid-1960s*

"Philosophy is just a hobby. You can't open a philosophy factory."

> *Dewey Selmon, on majoring in philosophy at the University of Oklahoma*

"It was like a heart transplant. We tried to implant college in him, but his head rejected it."

> *Barry Switzer, on why one of his players left college*

"Because I'm still about 30 credits short of getting my degree."

> *Jim Zorn, on why he was shocked when he was contacted by his alma mater, Cal Poly, about giving a keynote address*

COLOR MY WORLD

"I've watched them on film, but all I can remember is their uniforms were white on one film and dark on the other."

> *Lou Holtz, on playing West Virginia in the Fiesta Bowl*

COLTS

"They all ran fast. They all ran toward the ball. They all arrived in bad humor."

> *Bum Phillips, on the great defensive line of the Baltimore Colts of the mid-1970s*

COMEBACKS

"I'm bored, I'm broke, and I'm back."

> *John Riggins, on his comeback after sitting out the 1980 season*

CONTRACTS

"The first time I realized it was a nightmare was when I heard their salary demands."

> *Terry Bradshaw, on a dream in which he had 22 of football's all-time greats on his team*

"All coaches are in the last year of their contract, only some of them don't know it."

> *Dan Henning*

"A lifetime contract for a coach means if you're ahead in the third quarter and moving the ball, they can't fire you."

> *Lou Holtz*

"When I get depressed, I just go home and read my five-year contract."

> *Lou Holtz, on predictions of a bad season at Arkansas*

"On the basis of what they're offering, I could play four or five games."

> *John Riggins, during contract negotiations with the Redskins*

"I don't expect to win enough games to be put on NCAA probation. I just want to win enough to warrant an investigation."

Bob Devaney, Nebraska coach

"I've never seen anyone kick off so much."

Mike Gottfried, on a great
Nebraska team

"We just have to make enough to cover hospital expenses."

Lou Holtz, on his Minnesota team
facing Nebraska

"They're big. They're strong. They're fast. Their mothers love them. . . . And they'll kill you."

Jim Walden, Iowa State coach,
on Nebraska

"We used to go to the Holiday Bowl and our fans would bring a $50 dollar bill and the Ten Commandments and break neither."

> *LaVell Edwards, Brigham Young coach, on why his team never attracted enough attention at bowl time*

"They let you chase girls, they just don't let you catch them."

> *Glen Kozlowski, on playing college ball at BYU*

"Leaving."

> *Jim McMahon, on his fondest memory of BYU*

COUNTRY LIFE

"He and I are as country as two piles of cow manure in a barn."

Ken Stabler, on himself and
Bum Phillips

COWBOYS

"Buddy doesn't have many rules, but one of them is don't lose to the Cowboys."

Mike Golic, on Buddy Ryan when he
coached the Eagles

"We're as clean as any team. We wash our hands before we hit anybody."

Nate Newton, refuting charges that
the Cowboys were a dirty team

"He doesn't coach offense or defense. He watches the game and I guess he tells them when to take a penalty and when not."

Buddy Ryan, on Barry Switzer

"The game of football is Xs and Os. In their case, it should be O and X, which spells Ox."

Hank Stram, on the Cowboys' huge offensive line of 1995

"The first time we won three in a row and the NCAA didn't call to tell me we were under investigation."

Barry Switzer, on when he knew he was coaching the Cowboys

"At first, teams hated us out of respect for the Dallas Cowboys. Now they hate us out of disrespect."

Everson Walls, on many of the Cowboys crossing the picket line during the NFL strike

CRAZY LEGS

"You've heard of people who zig or zag. Well, Elroy also had a zog and a couple of zugs."

Norm Van Brocklin, on Elroy "Crazy Legs" Hirsch

CRICKET

"It's as exciting as mailing letters."
> *Pat Haden, on playing cricket while*
> *on his Rhodes scholarship*

CRIMSON TIDE

"He was so tough that he gave the captain ten laps if he lost the coin toss."
> *Frank Howard, on ex–Alabama*
> *coach Wallace Wade*

"It's somebody who loves his wife more than football."
> *Sonny Smith, former Alabama*
> *basketball coach, on the definition of*
> *an Alabama pervert*

CURFEW

"You usually wind up staying up all night, or until your best player comes in."

*John McKay, on why he never had
bed checks*

CSONK

"When Larry Csonka goes on safari, the lions roll up the window."

Monte Clark

AL DAVIS

"He's like an 80-year-old Fonzie."

Dennis Miller, on Al Davis

"Al Davis is the kind of guy who would steal your eyes and then try to convince you that you looked better without them."

Sam Rutigliano

DEATH BE NOT PROUD

"It'll say: 'To my wife—I told you I was sick.'"
> *Lou Holtz, on what he wants on*
> *his tombstone*

DEE—FENSE

"The good news is that our defense is giving up only one touchdown a game. The bad news is that our offense is doing the same."
> *Bobby Bowden, on Florida State*

"It's like comparing the Atlantic to the Pacific. You can drown in either one."
> *Jim Dickey, Kansas State University*
> *coach, comparing the defenses of*
> *top-ranked Nebraska and*
> *number-two Oklahoma*

"We're totally committed to defense. I'm not so sure our defense is committed to defense, but the rest of the team is."

*Lou Holtz, after a lousy defensive
game by Notre Dame*

"Tighten the loose ends and loosen the tight ends."

*Mike Singletary, describing the
defensive strategy of the Bears*

"Anybody can play offense, but it takes a man to play defense."

Bud Wilkinson

DEFENSIVE LINEMEN

"Now that I'm retired, I want to say that all defensive linemen are sissies."

Dan Fouts

"If their IQs were five points lower, they would be geraniums."

Russ Francis, on defensive linemen

"If you're mad at your kid, you can either raise him to be a nose tackle or send him out to play on the freeway. It's about the same."
Bob Golic

"If we win again, I didn't know if he would be strong enough to carry me off the field."
Lou Holtz, on deciding not to recruit a defensive lineman who didn't look very strong

"I just grab me an armful of men, pick 'em over until I find the one with the ball, then I throw him down."
Big Daddy Lipscomb, describing his style

"My job has become decoy. I draw the attack and the other guys make the plays. I should show up painted like a duck."
Howie Long

"A good defensive lineman has to be part buffalo and part ballet dancer."
Merlin Olsen

"Without Dickerson, the Rams are a pit bull with dentures."

> *Scott Ostler, on Dickerson's*
> *contract problems*

"He won't have any problem recognizing the game plan—Eric around right end, Eric around left end, Eric up the middle."

> *John Robinson, on Dickerson*
> *returning from a holdout*

DIET

"As soon as it's light, I start to eat."

> *Art Donovan, after saying he was a*
> *light eater*

"We've got Keeney on the lettuce diet. Unfortunately, he eats forty pounds of lettuce a day."

> *Steve Sloan, Texas Tech coach, on*
> *6'6", 335-pound Mike Keeney*

"It wasn't watching what I ate. It was watching what my friends ate."

Wilbur Young, Chargers lineman, on the toughest part of losing 85 pounds

DISCIPLINE

"My idea of discipline is not making guys do something, it's getting 'em to do it."
Bum Phillips

DISCOUNT CHAINS

"He looks like some guy we picked up from Wal-Mart."

Brett Favre, on 33-year-old tight end Ed West

DISSENSION
IN THE RANKS

"Everyone is unhappy at times, even my wife. Only she doesn't get interviewed about it."

> *John McKay, on Buccaneers players*
> *who were complaining to the press*

MIKE DITKA

"It was interesting playing tennis with Mike—at least as long as his racket lasted."

> *Tom Landry, on the temper of*
> *Mike Ditka*

"If I were the NFL commissioner, I'd put all the offensive linemen in jail for 30 days or make them spend one week with Mike Ditka."

> *Dexter Manley*

CONRAD DOBLER

"If I see him in the field with his back to the play, I'll cripple him. And if I saw him in the street tomorrow, I'd hurt his head."

Bubba Baker, on Dobler

DOCTOR, DOCTOR

"If I was smart enough to be a doctor, I'd be a doctor. I ain't, so I'm a football player."

Dick Butkus

"If I drop dead tomorrow, at least I'll know I died in good health."

Bum Phillips, after passing his physical

DOLPHINS

"One of the major achievements of my life was to get more than $100 million in debt."
Joe Robbie, on financing Joe Robbie Stadium

DON'T WORRY, BE HAPPY

"Am I happy? I never said I wasn't."
Duane Thomas, breaking his long silence after the Cowboys won the Super Bowl, when asked if he was happy

DOUBLE ZERO

"One thing Jim doesn't need is game experience."
John Madden, on Jim Otto missing an exhibition game after not missing a regular-season game for 15 years

"But now that it's me, it loses some of its mystique."

Drew Bledsoe, on the mystique surrounding the NFL's first draft pick

"It's like a beauty contest. It's easy to pick out the top one, two, or three girls; but then the rest of them look the same."

Gil Brandt, Cowboys vice president, on the NFL draft

"The scouts said I looked like Tarzan and played like Jane."

Dennis Harrison, a 6'8", 275-pounder, on being a fourth-round draft choice

"Whenever I look at the Jets' draft choices and see no guards among them, I consider that a real good draft."

Dave Herman, former New York Jets guard

"People say somewhere in the first round. Maybe even higher."

> *Craig "Ironhead" Heyward, on where he would be drafted*

"I think they drafted in alphabetical order."

> *Brent Ziegler, on being picked 265th in the draft*

DREAMS AND NIGHTMARES

"No, I dream about girls."

> *Dexter Clinkscale, asked if he ever dreamed that the Cowboys would give up 44 and 50 points in two consecutive games*

DROPS

"If he were the sky, he could probably drop the Goodyear blimp."

Dan Jenkins, on Fred Solomon dropping four passes in a game

DRUG TESTING

"They don't mind after they find out they don't have to study for it."

Mack Brown, former Tulane coach, on his players' reactions to drug testing

DRUGS

"That's like saying you're robbing a bank for fun."

Bum Phillips, on players who say they use cocaine for recreation

ECONOMICS

"At least I'm not a stockbroker."
>*Watson Brown, Vanderbilt coach, on*
>*losing a game 42–14 the same week*
>*as the stock market crash*

"My only request is that I draw my last dollar and my last breath at precisely the same instant."
>*Bobby Layne*

EGO

"If I were a reporter, I'd want to talk to me."
>*Todd Christianson, on breaking his*
>*silence with the media*

"If you don't have an ego, you're a wino."
>*Conrad Dobler*

"I'm surprised there wasn't a boycott or a march on downtown Dallas to protest it."

Thomas "Hollywood" Henderson, on being waived by the Cowboys

"There's only one thing you need to know. Throw the ball to '88.'"

Michael Irvin, number 88, advice he gave to Cowboys backup quarterback Hugh Millen

"If I didn't enjoy gloating so much, I probably wouldn't do as many interviews."

Jimmy Johnson

"He is unhappy everywhere except in his own arms."

Dave Kindred, on Eric Dickerson

JOHN ELWAY

"John certainly is one of the finest quarterbacks since Jack Kemp."

Newt Gingrich, on John Elway

"John Elway is an immediate cure for coach's burnout."

John Madden

"Since we're a one-man team, John Elway has a curfew. The rest can do what they want."

Dan Reeves, former Broncos coach

"John Elway is the master of the inconceivable pass thrown to the unreachable spot."

Pat Summerall

EMOTION

"Emotion disappears about the sixth time that guy hits you in the mouth and you realize those tears in your eyes are not because of dear old alma mater."

Bill Curry, former Alabama coach

"There was a lot of emotion at the Alamo, and nobody survived."

Ron Meyer, on how emotion is overrated on the football field

EXPERIENCE

"If you have everyone back from a team that lost 10 games, experience isn't too important."

John McKay, on the significance of experience

EYE CHART

"I recruited a Czech kicker, and during the eye examination the doctor asked if he could read the bottom line. The Czech kicker said, 'Read it? I know him.'"

Woody Hayes

FACIAL HAIR

"My mom says it's because I don't shave."

Brett Favre, on not getting as many endorsements as Troy Aikman

"I'll probably hear from his mother about that."
Fred Akers, Texas coach, on playing
everyone on the team except his
son Danny

"Football doesn't take me away from my family life.
We've always watched films together."
Fred Akers

"I know their mother—she'd give them all
my plays."
Bobby Bowden, on why he doesn't
want to play against his sons' teams

"The biggest benefit is having my parents here as
very accessible baby-sitters."
Bill Cowher, on the best part
of coaching in his hometown
of Pittsburgh

"They can't fire me because my family buys too
many tickets."
LaVell Edwards, BYU coach, on
being one of 14 children

"No—the next Barry Bonds."

> *Barry Foster, asked if he would*
> *like his newborn son to be the*
> *next Barry Foster*

"My teenage daughter has a new boyfriend. My son just made the basketball team in junior high school. And my wife found a tennis partner she can beat."

> *Lou Holtz, on why he was*
> *reluctant to leave the New York*
> *Jets coaching job*

"My father-in-law and I have a great deal in common. We both love football, golf, and his daughter—not necessarily in that order."

> *Lou Holtz*

"To me, football is a contest in embarrassments. The quarterback is out there to embarrass me in front of my friends, my teammates, my coach, my wife, and my three boys. The quarterback doesn't leave me any choice. I've got to embarrass him instead."

> *Alex Karras*

"If ESPN had been around 18 years ago, I wouldn't have any children."

> *Gene Murphy, Fullerton football*
> *coach, on his addiction to ESPN*

"I really don't know. I don't see her that much."

> *Ray Perkins, former Alabama coach,*
> *on what his wife thinks about his*
> *18-hour workdays*

"Really, I never tuteled that boy."

> *Bum Phillips, asked if he expected a*
> *reward for the tutelage he gave his*
> *son Wade*

"I'd just plead heredity."

> *Wade Phillips, NFL coach and son of*
> *Bum Phillips, asked what he would*
> *do if things went wrong*

"Every time I go to see my parents in Norway, they ask me what I'm going to do when I grow up."

> *Jan Stenerud, at age 38, on his long*
> *Hall of Fame career as a placekicker*

"I even got booed in the men's room."
Bobby Layne, after a bad game

"He's the guy who sits 40 rows up in the stands and wonders why a 17-year-old kid can't hit another 17-year-old kid with a ball from 40 yards away. Then he goes out to the parking lot and can't find his car."
Chuck Mills, former Wake Forest coach, defining a football fan

"I'm ready for anything. I've even brought birdseed for the boo birds."
Everson Walls, on a tough crowd expected at a Cowboys game

"I don't even go to self-service gasoline stations anymore because I don't want to have to walk in and pay for it."
Sam Wyche, former Bengals coach, on an 0–5 start to the season

FAN MAIL

"It was about three-to-one that I was not an SOB. But there were a lot of ones."

John McKay, on fan mail he received as Tampa Bay coach

FIELD GOALS

"Dempsey didn't kick that field goal. God did."

Wayne Walker, on Tom Dempsey's famous 63-yard field goal

FIGHTING IRISH

"Notre Dame is the only team in the country that never plays a road game."

Beano Cook, on all the Notre Dame fans around the country

"The three toughest jobs in the world are: president of the United States, mayor of New York, and head football coach at Notre Dame."

Beano Cook

"Russia in the winter and Notre Dame in South Bend."

Beano Cook, on the two things you never bet against

"If they retired the numbers of all the greats at Notre Dame, there wouldn't be any numbers left."

Terry Hanratty, asked if his number should be retired

"At a Christian school, you don't talk about revenge."

Lou Holtz, asked if beating Stanford by 28 points was revenge for losing to them the prior year

"It's like you've got termites and you're trying to sell the house. You know there's termites, but the guy buying the house doesn't."

Lou Holtz, on trying to hide Notre Dame's deficiencies

"A patient of Dr. Kevorkian has a better future than I do."

Lou Holtz, on leaving Notre Dame

"This is the first place I've been where I haven't had to sell tickets."

Lou Holtz, on taking the Notre Dame coaching job

"You don't ask a president of a small company to become chairman of the board of General Motors."

Ara Parseghian, on the unsuccessful coaching reign of former high school football coach Gerry Faust

"I don't think you can keep Notre Dame fans around the country happy unless you win every game by 35 points."

Joe Paterno, on Lou Holtz never getting the credit he deserved

"I won't know until my barber tells me on Monday."

Knute Rockne, asked why Notre Dame lost a game

"I beg your pardon. I thought this was a Notre Dame team."

Knute Rockne, commenting to his players at halftime in a game Notre Dame was losing

"We believe in the spirit of Notre Dame, but some people think it's false. I understand their point. If we are so blessed, then why did we go 5–6 in 1985?"

Mike Stonebreaker

"At some schools, hope springs eternal. Here, demand springs eternal."

Larry Williams

FIGHTS

"It is never a good fight when a little guy meets a great big guy, particularly since the little guy in this case was me."

Walt Garrison, on fighting with defensive end Bob Lurtsema

"We've already got sudden death—but only for the coaches who lose."

> *Al Conover, Rice coach, on the*
> *implementation of sudden death*

"The fat lady might have cleared her throat, but she hasn't sung yet."

> *Spike Dykes, Texas Tech coach,*
> *after his team lost five of its first*
> *six games*

"When I die, the Lord is going to have a lot of questions—but so am I."

> *Dan Henning, on being fired as Lions*
> *offensive coordinator*

"Coaching is nothing more than eliminating mistakes before you get fired."

> *Lou Holtz*

"One of my biggest goals is not to get fired."

> *Larry Lacewell, former Arkansas*
> *State coach, on being asked his goals*
> *when he was hired*

"If your work is not fired with enthusiasm, you will be fired—with enthusiasm."

John Mazur, former Patriots coach

"Capece is kaput."

John McKay, on releasing kicker
Bill Capece

"There are two types of coaches. The kind that have just been fired and the kind that are going to get fired."

Bum Phillips

"It means I can be fired from two jobs instead of one."

Dan Reeves, on being named
both vice president and coach of
the Broncos

"I'm the only coach in history to go straight from the White House to the outhouse."

Pepper Rodgers, fired as Georgia
Tech coach the day after he met
President Carter at the White House

FOOD

"I had frog legs for my appetizer. That's why I'm so jumpy this morning."

> *Nate Newton, on a meal he had the night before the Super Bowl*

"There ain't but four things in life I know somethin' about—pickup trucks, gumbo, cold beer, and barbecued ribs."

> *Bum Phillips*

FOOTBALL BASHERS

"If a man watches three football games in a row, he should be declared legally dead."

> *Erma Bombeck*

"Baseball players are smarter than football players. How often do you see a baseball team punished for too many men on the field?"

> *Jim Bouton*

"They do one-armed push-ups so they can count with their other hand."

Al McGuire, on football players

"The football season is like pain. You forget how terrible it is until it seizes you again."

Sally Quinn

"Football features two of the worst aspects of American life—violence and committee meetings."

George Will

"The UN is just like football—a series of huddles always followed by outbursts of violence."

George Will

FOOTBALL WISDOM

"Football is a wonderful way to get rid of aggressiveness without going to jail for it."

Heywood Hale Broun

"Football isn't a contact sport—it's a collision sport. Dancing is a contact sport."
Duffy Daugherty

"You can learn more character on the two-yard line than you can anywhere in life."
Paul Dietzel, former Army coach

"If you ever forget football is a violent game, they'll catch you gazing at the stars and put your lights out."
Conrad Dobler

"Pro football is like nuclear warfare. There are no winners—only survivors."
Frank Gifford

"I'd catch a punt naked in the snow in Buffalo for a chance to play in the NFL."
Steve Hendrickson, University of California player, on how desperate he was to get into the NFL

"I don't mind starting the season with unknowns. I just don't like finishing the season with them."
Lou Holtz

"The man who complains about the way the ball bounces is likely the one who dropped it."
Lou Holtz

"We try to hurt everybody. We hurt each other as hard as we can. This is a man's game."
Sam Huff

"Football is blocking and tackling. Everything else is mythology."
Vince Lombardi

"If you play one regular-season game in the National Football League, you will never, ever, be normal physically."
John Madden

"Football's a great life. Just think . . . they pay you good money to eat well, stay in shape, and have fun."
Hugh McElhenny

"We'll have an offensive team and a defensive team. And the other team will be in charge of carrying me off the field."

John McKay, on playing a game with only a small number of players

"All the computers and all the genius coaches aren't worth a damn on Sunday if they don't have a bunch of tough guys who go out and play like somebody called their mama a bad name."

Steve McMichael

"Tennis is like football. You must set up the plays. If you set it up right, all you have to do is execute."

Martina Navratilova

"The kind who would just nod their heads, pack their bags, and be early if I told 'em we had a game in some shopping-center parking lot, for no money, at 6 A.M. some Wednesday morning."

Bill Parcells, describing parking-lot players

"Two kinds of football players ain't worth a damn. One that never does what he's told and the other that does nothing except what he's told."
Bum Phillips

"Potential will get you beat 21–7 every time."
Bum Phillips

"There are two ways to build a team. You either get better players or get the players you've got to play better."
Bum Phillips

"If you're a lineman, you have to be big and dumb. If you're a back, you only have to be dumb."
Knute Rockne

"Football is a game played with arms and legs and shoulders, but mainly from the neck up."
Knute Rockne

"Football doesn't build character. It eliminates the weak ones."
Darrell Royal

"Only angry people win football games."
Darrell Royal

"The object of football is not to annihilate the other team, but to advance the ball."
Clark Shaughnessy, Stanford coach

"The game of football is to college life what color is to painting. It makes college life throb and vibrate."
Bob Zuppke

49ERS

"If we played Cucamonga High School right now, it would be a tough game."
Ronnie Lott, on a great 49ers team going through a cold streak

"They don't have Keith's time in the 40 because he's never gone that far."

Don Criqui, on 6'5", 320-pound replacement player Keith Bosley

"Shorts."

Chuck Doyle, Holy Cross football player, asked what he ran the 40 in

"I'm probably about a 4.9 normally, but when a 280-pound guy is chasing me—I'm a 4.6."

John Elway, on the 40-yard dash

"The fastest 40 yards I ever ran."

Gary Fencik, Bears player, on running with the bulls in Pamplona

"They know how fast I am. I ran past their secondary enough times."

Dennis McKinnon, free-agent wide receiver, on refusing to run a 40-yard dash for the Eagles

FREE AGENTS

"You don't go from a Yugo to a Benz back to a Yugo."

> *Deion Sanders, on the possibility of going back to the Falcons as a free agent after a year with the 49ers*

FRESHMAN YEAR

"The best time to play a freshman is when he is a junior."

> *Cal Stoll, former Minnesota football coach*

FRIDGE

"It's a good thing William Perry doesn't need it. They'd have had to use a harpoon."

> *Buddy Baron, discussing Jim McMahon's acupuncture before the 1986 Super Bowl*

"He bench-presses the gymnasium."

Jerry Claiborne, Kentucky coach,
on William Perry's college days
at Clemson

"It's like trying to cut down a moving
lumber yard."

George Cumby, on blocking
William "The Refrigerator" Perry

"About 310 pounds, eyes of blue, about the cutest
thing you ever saw."

Mike Ditka, on "The Fridge"

"They've got a movie on his life coming out. It's
called 'The Endorser.'"

Dan Hampton, on all of William
Perry's endorsements

"When you go in, carry an elephant gun with you."

Dennis Johnson, on the best way to
stop William Perry from scoring

"William Perry is a meal away from being a
pigeon's best friend."

Bernie Lincicome

FRIENDS TO THE END

"This Thanksgiving I called all of my friends in the league. It took about 12 seconds."
Jerry Glanville

"I think his two best friends were one of the ball boys and, I think, a retired equipment manager."
Bobby Hebert, on Jeff George's popularity with the Falcons players

"It's good to have friends, but you want to beat them just like you do your enemies."
Buddy Ryan

TONI FRITSCH

"Fritsch is so good, he practices missin'."
Bum Phillips, on kicker Toni Fritsch

"Every time I look up and see that kid on the field, I thank God for the immigration laws."
Bum Phillips

FUMBLES

"The only way I know to cut down on our fumbles is to punt on first down every series. Even then, we might fumble the snap."

> *Barry Switzer, on an Oklahoma team that fumbled a great deal*

GAMBLIN' MAN

"Munson hasn't done anything wrong. I'd bet my house on it."

> *Joe Schmidt, after Bill Munson was asked to testify in a gambling inquiry*

GAS ATTACK

"It's an internal matter."

> *Bill Walsh, on reports about Russ Francis missing a practice due to a stomach bug*

GENERAL MANAGER

"I thought maybe I was going to be a general manager because I kept wanting to take a nap."
Jerry Glanville, on being sick with pneumonia

GET A LIFE

"If we didn't have a huddle, Jim would have no social life."
Phil Simms, on teammate Jim Burt

GIANTS

"It's like playing against a jailbreak."
Mike Ditka, on the Giants' great linebacking core of Lawrence Taylor, Harry Carson, and Carl Banks

GOIN' OUT OF MY HEAD

"To keep Greg Bingham out of a game, you'd have to cut off his head and then hide it. Just cuttin' off his head wouldn't accomplish anything. He'd find it and try to play anyway."

Bum Phillips, on linebacker
Greg Bingham

GOLDEN BOY

"Paul Hornung was an impact player for the Packers. He was also an impact player to half the females in the USA."

Max McGee, on Paul Hornung

GOLF GAME

"I guess the first time I three-putt."

Mike Ditka, asked when he would
start to think about the following
season after winning the Super Bowl

"All my life I've been trying to make a hole in one. The closest I ever came was a bogey."
Lou Holtz

"There is one big difference. You're standing still in golf. Stand still in football and you're dead."
Hale Irwin, on the difference between golf and football

"My best score ever was 103. But I've only been playing 15 years."
Alex Karras, on golf

"Not if he can swing a golf club."
Joe Montana, asked if he wanted his son to play football

"I refuse to spend an afternoon in April watching Marino and Elway square off on the 18th tee, locked atop the leaders board at 16 above."
Ed Shiffer, football writer, on a proposed Pro Athlete Golf League

"The only thing I'm worried about is getting the left hand steady, then hitting it straight."
Lawrence Taylor, on his retirement

"I like golf because I can go out and hit a little white ball that doesn't move and doesn't hit back. It should be easy, but it isn't."

Lawrence Taylor

"Don't blame me. Blame the foursome ahead of me."

Lawrence Taylor, on being late for a Giants practice

GOPHERS

"Anytime your defense gives up more points than your basketball team, you're in trouble."

Lou Holtz, on his days at the University of Minnesota

GRADUATION DAY

"I plan to attend his graduation."

> *Dan McCann, Duquesne coach, on*
> *Georgetown junior Jim Corcoran,*
> *after Duquesne lost for the second*
> *straight year on a Corcoran field goal*

GRAMBLIN' MAN

"They're everywhere—under the beds, in the closets, even in the bathroom closet."

> *Doris Robinson, wife of Eddie*
> *Robinson, on what he's done with all*
> *his trophies and awards*

"When the boys get in trouble and are told they can make one phone call, they use it to call me."

> *Eddie Robinson, legendary*
> *Grambling coach*

RED GRANGE

"If you can't explain it, how can you take credit for it?"

> *Red Grange, on his ability to elude tacklers*

"Three or four men and a horse rolled into one."
> *Damon Runyon, describing Grange*

"He is Jack Dempsey, Babe Ruth, Al Jolson, Paavo Nurmi, and Man O' War."
> *Damon Runyon, describing Grange*

MEAN JOE GREENE

"You come out hurting all over, and what didn't hurt didn't work."
> *Jim Otto, on facing Joe Greene*

"Joe Greene was on *Wild Kingdom* once, and they shot him."
> *Don Rickles*

HAIR IT IS

"Bald State."

> *Barry Bennett, on the alma mater of*
> *bald placekicker Garo Yepremian*

"Just once I would like to run and feel the wind in my hair."

> *Rocky Bleier, imagining what it*
> *would be like to have hair*

"It's not the legs that go first—it's the hair."
> *Pat Leahy, Jets placekicker, at*
> *age 40*

"I want little conversation and lots of hair on the floor."

> *Bum Phillips, on what he expects*
> *from a barber*

"Somewhere in Detroit, there's a helmet with all my hair in it."

> *Wayne Walker, retired Lions*
> *linebacker, explaining his loss of hair*

"I'd run down the field with my hair on fire—
naked—just to get back in uniform."

> *Jamie Williams, 49ers tight end who*
> *was on the disabled list*

HALFTIME SPEECH

"I wish I could remember my halftime speech so I
could forget it."

> *Jerry Davitch, Idaho football coach,*
> *on losing to Weber State 42–21 after*
> *leading at halftime 21–14*

"I guess after the half our players forget the game
plan and do what they think is best."

> *Lou Holtz, on why his Arkansas team*
> *plays best in the third quarter*

"I give the same halftime speech over and over. It
works best when my players are better than the
other coaches' players."

> *Chuck Mills*

HANGMAN

"I'm glad it happened in front of the library. I've always emphasized scholarship."

> *Doug Weaver, former Kansas State University coach, on being hanged in effigy near the library*

JOHN HANNAH

"You take a gun and shoot him before the game."

> *Jim Haslett, on the best way to handle legendary guard John Hannah*

JIM HARBAUGH

"You can have the fancy-dan quarterbacks. Patton would have been proud of him; Schwarzkopf would have loved him. He might be America's quarterback."

> *Mike Ditka, on the heroic play of Jim Harbaugh*

FRANCO HARRIS

"Franco Harris faked me out so bad one time
that I got a 15-yard penalty for grabbing my
own face mask."

D. D. Lewis

HAWKEYES

"He's great to be around, but keep a hand on
your billfold."

Spike Dykes, on Iowa coach Hayden
Fry, who has a reputation as a
con man

WOODY HAYES

"When I look in the mirror in the morning,
I want to take a swing at me."

Woody Hayes, on his
combative personality

HEAT IS ON

"If God wanted it so hot, why did he invent
people?"

> *Claude Humphrey, on hot weather at*
> *a preseason practice*

HEIGHT REPORT

"He doesn't shine his shoes, he drives them
through a car wash."

> *Earle Bruce, on 6'4" offensive tackle*
> *Mark Krerowicz, who wears size*
> *16 shoes*

"I used to be 6'7"; I lost half an inch. Too many
goal-line stands."

> *Dave Butz, defensive lineman*

"It's good to have a lineman you can look straight
in the belly button."

> *Larry Csonka, on 6'6", 285-pound*
> *Gordon King*

"They have either the biggest linemen I've ever seen or the smallest buildings I've ever seen."
Tony DeMeco, Iona football coach, on an opponent

"He leaves plenty of room in the huddle."
Gordon King, on why the 5'7" Joe Morris was a welcome addition to the Giants' huddle

"I don't treat little people like poodles just because they're little. Why should people treat me like an ape in a cage because I'm big?"
Howie Long

"He's so short, his breath smells of earthworms."
Ron Meyer, Southern Methodist University coach, on 5'7" Harvey McAtee

"When he's covered, he's open."
Ron Meyer, on 6'8" tight end Robert Hubble

"You know, at the circus—they bring those little cars in and 18 guys get out. He'd be in that group."

Bill Parcells, on 5'8" Giants wide receiver Stephen Baker

"He's not small, he's just short."

Bum Phillips, on 5'9", 200-pound running back Horace Belton

"We put in a special formation for him—the sawed-off shotgun."

Mike Tomczak, on 5'9" quarterback Doug Flutie

HEISMAN TROPHY

"I still think the majority of people who vote for the award are like the people in Congress—not very bright."

Beano Cook, on the people who vote for the Heisman Trophy

"If I sit out another year, I'll probably get the Heisman Trophy."

> *Tim Marshall, on being named to the 1983 preseason All-American team after sitting out the 1982 season with an injury*

"I don't have room for it. It'd just be something else I'd have to dust."

> *Hattie Walker, Vagas Ferguson's grandmother, on the possibility of the Notre Dame running back winning the Heisman Trophy*

HIGH SCHOOL DAYS

"I should know something about it. As a juvenile, I was a delinquent."

> *Craig Heyward, on studying criminal justice in college, with a specialty in juvenile delinquency*

"When I hit a guy, I wanted him to know who hit him without his even having to look around and check a number."

Dick Butkus

"When I hit a guy, I'll hit him in the throat—he doesn't have pads on his throat."

Conrad Dobler

HOCKEY

"We were throwing interceptions and they were running for touchdowns."

Bob Johnson, former Calgary Flames coach, on losing a hockey game 7–1

HOG WILD

"I was like a hog going after a sweet potato in the mud."

Kevin Greene, after a great game

HOGS

"I'm a construction-worker type. I want to go to work, eat my lunch, work some more, go to a bar and have a beer, and go home and eat."

Russ Grimm, describing his role as chief Hog on the famous Redskins offensive line

"The really scary thing is that some of these people work for the government."

Joe Jacoby, on Redskins fans showing up for games in pig snouts

"I think they're a bunch of slobs, but they're my kind of people."

John Riggins, on the Hogs

HOLD ME

"It taught me how to hold good."

> *Ron Essink, Seahawks offensive*
> *lineman, on wrestling in college*

"They're used to being held all the time."

> *Lou Holtz, on why big linemen are*
> *so secure*

"Of course we hold. We're getting older, and it's a lot easier than blocking."

> *Bubba Paris, asked if he ever held*

"You have to be big and have a good grip."

> *Jack Reynolds, on what it takes*
> *to be a good offensive lineman*

HOMECOMING

"We get no respect. Everybody we play on the road
has made us their homecoming game."

*Lee Corso, former Indiana
University coach*

HOOPS

"The football team outscored us."

*Dave Bliss, former Oklahoma
basketball coach, on a low-scoring
Oklahoma team*

"I think basketball would be his first love simply
because he can live longer."

*Bobby Bowden, on why he would
recommend that Charlie Ward play
basketball over football*

"I never finished a basketball game. I always fouled
out. I had more fouls, I think, than the second
string had points."

Conrad Dobler

"If I was going to get beat up, I wanted it to be indoors where it was warm."

> *Tom Heinsohn, on why he chose basketball over football*

HOOSIERS

"They wanted to send me over there too, but with a one-way ticket."

> *Lee Corso, former Indiana football coach, on Indiana basketball coach Bobby Knight getting an all-expense-paid trip to Europe*

HORSE SENSE

"Never again will I invest in anything that eats."

> *Jay Hilgenberg, on investing in racehorses*

"The horses have no agents, they don't call me in the morning to renegotiate after winning a race, they don't petition me for more oats, and they don't object to urine analysis."

Gene Klein, on going from owning the Chargers to owning horses

"He's a marvelous animal. He didn't even ask to renegotiate."

Bum Phillips, on his two-year-old racehorse winning its first race

HUDDLE

"If you want a messenger, call Western Union."

Joe Don Looney, on the coach asking him to send in a play from the sidelines

HUNKS

"My wife hasn't said too much about it—since she stopped rolling on the floor laughing."

Joe Ferguson, on the 39-year-old being rated one of America's sexiest men

HURRICANES

"They look so good to me. I'm amazed they're not on strike."

Bobby Bowden, Florida State coach, on playing the University of Miami during the NFL strike

"I'd make sure my car was hidden."

Dennis Erickson, former Miami coach, on what he would do if Miami's 57-game home winning streak was broken

"It's like shopping with your grandmother. You hurry up and wait."

> *Brian Bosworth, on his slow recovery*
> *from an injury*

"What is a medium collateral whatever ligament? It sounds like spaghetti with meat sauce."

> *Art Donovan, making fun of the*
> *injuries of current players*

"I never could figure out why I was always breaking my hand. When you get hurt, you want to be carried off the field on a stretcher. Me, I always walked off holding my pinky."

> *Pat Haden*

"Ever since they put it in, I've been getting reception on my car radio."

> *Bob Kuechenberg, on the steel pin in*
> *his right arm*

"We just have to take our belt and tighten it another notch. I think I'm down to an 18-inch waist."

> *George McIntyre, Vanderbilt coach,*
> *on losing his seventh starter to injury*
> *early in the season*

"He's gonna be a great lineman, unless he gets hurt. And if he does, I'd like to have the guy who does it."

> *Bum Phillips, on Charles Philyaw*

"I'm running out of spare parts."

> *Jim Plunkett, on his many injuries*

"We've decided to take the team picture this year in the trainer's room."

> *Bubba Tyer, Redskins trainer, on all*
> *the injuries suffered by the Redskins*

INSURANCE POLICIES

"It was the same story everyplace I went. I was the guy they kept for insurance. They should have dressed me up in a policy instead of a uniform."

Jack Kemp, on his early days in football

"These are the games that make you want to sell insurance."

Tom Olivadotti, Dolphins defensive coordinator, on the Dolphins giving up more than 550 yards to the Bills

INTELLIGENCE TESTS

"You have to be stupid, and that's working out well for me."

Bubba Baker, on what it takes to play in the NFL

"He doesn't know the meaning of the word fear. In fact I just saw his grades, and he doesn't know the meaning of a lot of words."

Bobby Bowden, on Reggie Herring

"Well, Rolf, do you want to kick with the wind or against it?"

Don Coryell, said to placekicker Rolf Benirschke before a game at the Seattle Kingdome

"The NFL, like life, is full of idiots."
Randy Cross

"Sometimes God gives you physical talents and takes away your brain."

Mike Ditka, on Tim Harris

"Physically, he's a world-beater. Mentally, he's an eggbeater."

Matt Elliott, on Alonzo Spellman

"The hit movie of the summer was *Forrest Gump*, the heartwarming tale of a simpleminded Southern boy who leads a fantasy sports life. I kind of wished they had stuck with the original title, though: *The Terry Bradshaw Story*."
> *Russ Francis*

"How do you know what it's like to be stupid if you've never been smart?"
> *Lou Holtz*

"It was so tight, I had trouble thinking."
> *Danny Reed, 6'7", 400-pound high school football player, on having helmet problems*

INTERCEPTIONS

"I was too tired."
> *Louis Breeden, on why he didn't spike the ball after an interception and 102-yard touchdown return*

"I hope one of my senior quarterbacks is drawn, so the pie will be intercepted before it gets to my face."

Gary Fallon, Washington and Lee coach, before a drawing to determine which player would throw a pie in his face for charity

"We need to make a tackle chart for our offense."

David McWilliams, Texas coach, after his quarterbacks threw seven interceptions in a game

"Wehrli's become one of my best receivers."

Roger Staubach, after St. Louis Cardinals defensive back Roger Wehrli intercepted three Staubach passes

"Yeah—how to tackle."

Cliff Stoudt, asked if he learned anything after throwing three interceptions in a game

"It has been my experience that the fastest man on the football field is the quarterback who has just had his pass intercepted."

Barry Switzer

JETS

"They're the best 1–8 team I've seen."

Drew Bledsoe, on the 1996 New York Jets, who were on their way to a 1–15 season

"These Jets players are pretty confident. Like today, they said they plan to win a game next year, too."

Jay Leno, on the Jets' 1–15 season

"The New York Jets have been given permission to sell Girl Scout cookies."

David Letterman, on 12 teams being told they had permission to sell Super Bowl tickets just after the regular season ended

"I don't know if that's an honor."

Adrian Murrell, on being the first
player in 25 years to gain more than
a thousand yards for a team that
won only one game

JOB TO DO

"To me football is like a day off. I grew up picking cotton on my daddy's farm, and nobody asked for your autograph or put your name in the paper for that."

Lee Roy Jordan

"I try to play golf at least once a day."

Darrell Royal, on his responsibilities
as special assistant to the president of
the University of Texas

JOHNNY U

"I'm not sure he ever had a bad game. Maybe he had a bad half."

Raymond Berry, on Johnny Unitas

"He was the boss. He didn't have to holler or scream. It was just, 'Get John the ball, and he'll win.'"

Art Donovan

JIMMY JOHNSON

"If my hair can look better than his, I'll have it made."

Mike Ditka, on Jimmy Johnson

"That's impossible. It takes him 12 hours to comb his hair."

Jerry Glanville, on Jimmy Johnson's claim that he works 18 hours a day as the Cowboys coach

CHARLIE JOINER

"He deserves all the accolades he hasn't gotten."
Lester Hayes, on the vastly
underrated Charlie Joiner

DEACON JONES

"I'm the greatest defensive end around. I'd hate to have to play against me."
Deacon Jones

JERRY JONES

"Jerry wants a lot of things. In fact, Jerry wants everything."
Jimmy Johnson

"He flew into town in his own cargo plane, the only aircraft big enough to accommodate his carry-on ego."

Scott Ostler, on Jones flying into
Phoenix for Super Bowl XXX

JUICE

"You go for something you think is there, and all of a sudden you don't have anything."

Edgar Chandler, on O. J. Simpson

"I keep a picture of O. J. Simpson at my side at all times to remind me of the days when I knew how to coach."

John McKay, reminiscing about his
days coaching USC prior to the awful
early years as the Buccaneers' coach

"He doesn't belong to a union. Anyway, the ball doesn't weigh that much."

John McKay, on Simpson carrying
the ball 47 times in a game at USC

"What I want to know is, if this guy can fly, why does he need to rent a car?"

> *Reggie Rucker, on O. J. Simpson's*
> *Hertz commercials in which he*
> *"flew" through an airport*

ALEX KARRAS

"Karras has a lot of class. And all of it is third."

> *Conrad Dobler, on Alex Karras*

KICKERS

"You better produce now, or a month from now the developing will be done when you're working for Kodak."

> *Kevin Butler, on the immense*
> *pressure on kickers to produce*
> *immediate results*

"The two most important jobs in America are held by foreigners—room service and field-goal kicking."

> *Beano Cook*

"Our kicker had only one bad day last year—Saturday."

Gary Darnell, Tennessee Tech coach,
coming off an 0–11 season

"Never worry about missing a field goal. Just blame the holder and think about kicking the next one."
Lou Groza

"I didn't even think kickers were eligible."

Mark Mosley, on being named the
Associated Press Player of the Year
for 1982

"A collection of Walter Mittys: ordinary guys who dream about winning games for their teams. The difference is that it happens for field-goal kickers."
Jim Turner

THE KING

"I hear Elvis is living now in Michigan or Minnesota. Well, we'd like him to come and be on our bench. We don't care how much he weighs."

> *Jerry Glanville, on leaving tickets for Elvis Presley before a 1988 exhibition game in Memphis*

"I haven't heard from Elvis since his daughter married Michael Jackson. I think it killed him."

> *Jerry Glanville*

KNEE—JERK REACTION

"I've had all the stitches color-coded so the autopsy will be easier for everybody."

> *Dan Hampton, on his tenth knee operation*

"Most people have their ligaments and cartilage inside their knees. I keep mine on the top of my locker."

> *Joe Namath*

BERNIE KOSAR

"I've had loose change move around in the pocket better than Bernie."

Tom Zenner, sportscaster, on Bernie Kosar's lack of speed

JACK LAMBERT

"Why, Jack's so mean he doesn't even like himself."
Joe Greene

"I don't care for the man. He makes more money than I do, and he don't have no teeth. He's Dracula."

Thomas Henderson, on Lambert

TOM LANDRY

"I don't know—I only played there nine years."
Walt Garrison, asked if Tom Landry ever smiled

"Don't bother reading it, kid—everybody gets killed in the end."

> *Peter Gent, telling a rookie not to read the Cowboys' playbook*

"That's one way to look at it. The other is that I haven't had a promotion in 21 years."

> *Tom Landry, on entering his 21st season as the Cowboys' coach*

"He's such a perfectionist that if he were married to Dolly Parton, he'd expect her to cook."

> *Don Meredith, on Landry*

"We had many discussions, but I wasn't listening."

> *Don Meredith, on his many conversations with Landry*

"This is something that probably doesn't happen in Tom Landry's office."

> *Sam Wyche, on the Bengals' team cat vomiting in his office*

"During the week I practiced law. On Sunday,
I was the law."

> *Tommy Bell, NFL referee*
> *and attorney*

"You either have to finesse 12 people who weren't
smart enough to get out of jury duty, or 11 who
weren't smart enough to play offense."

> *Steve Fuller, Clemson quarterback,*
> *on deciding between football and*
> *law school*

"The NFL always loses in court. The NFL is the
Red Klotz of jurisprudence."

> *Tony Kornheiser*

"He'll be the first quarterback in history to play
three quarters and be able to bill them for four."

> *Jay Leno, on Steve Young going to*
> *law school in the off-season*

"That's kind of ironic, don't you think? Here's a guy who was an All-American football star in college. Then when he gets a job, he spends 30 years sitting on a bench."

> *Jay Leno, on Supreme Court Justice*
> *Byron "Whizzer" White*

BOBBY LAYNE

"When Bobby said block, you blocked. When Bobby said drink, you drank."

> *Yale Lary, on Bobby Layne*

"He stays out late, he visits interesting places, and he tips great."

> *Don Meredith, on why in his next life*
> *he'd like to be Bobby Layne's*
> *chauffeur*

"Bobby never lost a game. Some days, time just ran out on him."

> *Doak Walker*

LIFE ON THE FARM

"When I'm traveling, I ask farm boys how to get to a certain place. If they point with their fingers, I move on. If they pick up the plow and point with it, I stop and sell them on the University of Minnesota."

Gil Dobic

LINEBACKERS

"I want to be the hitter, not the hittee."

Charles Barkley, on why he wanted to be a professional linebacker

"Playing middle linebacker is like walking through a lion's cage in a three-piece pork-chop suit."

Cecil Johnson

"Playing middle linebacker is sort of a science. The key factor is to make an instantaneous response to a given stimulus."

Willie Lanier

"We're more aggressive, more mobile, and more smarter."

> *Greg Lloyd, on why the Steelers had*
> *better linebackers than the Bears*

"He's not twins."

> *John McKay, on the weaknesses of*
> *linebacker Hugh Green*

LIONS

"When I drive the fans still wave to me, and all of their fingers show."

> *Wayne Fontes, claiming his job as*
> *Lions coach was not in jeopardy*

"We had 100 percent attendance at all parties."

> *Bobby Layne, on leading the*
> *Detroit Lions to victory at parties*
> *as well as games*

"Coach Lombardi is very fair. He treats us all like dogs."

Henry Jordan

"In five days, I learned more from him than I had in 12 years of pro football."

Sonny Jurgensen, on Lombardi

"Lombardi was a cruel, kind, tough, gentle, miserable, wonderful man who I often hate and often love and always respect."

Jerry Kramer

"The quality of a man's life is in direct proportion to his commitment to excellence, regardless of his chosen field of endeavor."

Vince Lombardi

"When we go to a party, the hostess is still in the shower."

Mrs. Vince Lombardi, on his punctuality

"When he said sit down, I didn't even bother to look for a chair."

Max McGee

"When you played for Lombardi, anything other than death was a minor injury."

Bart Starr

LONGHORNS

"If Texas played the University of Iran, I'd be there with a big poster of the Ayatollah."

Dickie Griggs, former Texas Tech player, on how much he hated the University of Texas

"The University of Texas has only two major sports—football and spring football."

Jones Ramsey, University of Texas public information officer

LOOKS MAKE THE MAN

"I can't wait until tomorrow. Why not? 'Cause I get better looking every day."
Joe Namath

LOSING

"It is better to be devoured by lions than eaten by dogs."

Alex Agase, on believing in playing a tough schedule as Purdue coach

"I feel like the guy in the javelin competition who won the toss and elected to receive."

Mack Brown, former Tulane coach, on a 1–3 record

"It was a building year, but the building caved in on me."

Nick Coso, on his team's 0–8 record at Ferris State

"We have been like a guy trying to sell a set of encyclopedias. We have been in the house and everybody was excited, but we hadn't made the sale."

> *Wally English, former Tulane coach,*
> *on losing several close games midway*
> *through the season*

"What am I supposed to do? I can't open a new can of players."

> *Chuck Fairbanks, after losing his first*
> *game as a pro head coach with the*
> *Patriots*

"The sun doesn't shine on the same hound dog's rump every day."

> *Hayden Fry, Iowa coach, on being*
> *upset by Iowa State*

"I'll tell you what trouble is. It's when your admissions director, who is an alumnus of your opponent, sits on the opposite side of the field for the game and not with your own fans."

> *Vic Gatto, Tufts coach, on an*
> *0–7–1 record*

"It's hard to believe, but the score started at 0–0."

Dennis Green, former Northwestern
coach, on losing a game 64–0
to Iowa

"There's only one bright side of losing—the phone doesn't ring as much the following week."

Lou Holtz

"Welcome to the *Lou Holtz Show*. Unfortunately, I'm Lou Holtz."

Lou Holtz, opening his weekly TV
show in Arkansas after the
Razorbacks lost a game 31–7

"We definitely will be improved this year. Last year we lost 10 games. This year we only scheduled nine."

Ray Jenkins, former Montana
State coach

"I'd rather be a football coach. That way you only lose 11 games a year."

Abe Lemons, longtime college
basketball coach

"Last night I sat down and tried to think about the highlights from last year and I fell asleep."

Tom Lovatt, Utah coach, on a
1–10 season

"They say losing builds character. I have all the character I need."

Ray Malavasi

"It eats away at me like a vulture gnawing on some roadkill."

Steve McMichael, on losing

"When you see that big zero up there for wins, it's like somebody put a dead rat in your mouth."

Ron Meyer, Colts coach, after an
0–4 start

"The way we're playing, it would be a key game if we played Boy Scout Troop 180."

Don Morton, Wisconsin football coach

"It's not whether you win or lose, but who gets the blame."

Blaine Nye

"Show me a gracious loser and I'll show you a failure."

Knute Rockne

"They'll fire you for losing before they'll fire you for cheating."

Darryl Rogers

"If lessons are learned in defeat, our team is getting a good education."

Murray Warmath, Minnesota coach

"Our strong safety hurt his shoulder in the locker room raising his arm to say 'Charge.'"

Bill Yung, Texas–El Paso coach, on a bad year

RONNIE LOTT

"You don't need a tape measure to register his hits, you need a seismograph."

Jim Murray, on Ronnie Lott

LOVE AND MARRIAGE

"I don't want nobody who looks worse than me."
                    Richard Dent, on his marriage plans

"Divorce, no. Murder, yes."
                    Anne Hayes, asked if she ever
                    contemplated leaving her
                    husband Woody

LOVE AND ROMANCE

"I've dated girls who were far better looking than
the quality of the girls who should be going out
with me."
                    Cris Collinsworth, on the advantages
                    of being an NFL player

"I would still rather score a touchdown than make
love to the prettiest girl in the U.S."
                    Paul Hornung

"We call him Don Juan. The girls don juan him."
Bob Menko, on Cris Collinsworth

LUCK OF THE DRAW

"Luck is what happens when preparation meets opportunity."
Darrell Royal

JOHN MADDEN

"He's one man who doesn't let success get to his clothes."
Mike Ditka, on John Madden

MALAPROPS AND
FRACTURED SYNTAX

"I'm going to give 110 percent on every play. You can't give any more than that."

Jimmy Johnson, Illinois quarterback,
prior to the 1995 season

"He grew up on Rodeo Drive—in Hollywood."

Mark Jones, announcer, on
Wyoming player David Saraf,
from Beverly Hills

"The largest crowd ever in the state of Las Vegas."

Mark Jones, announcing the
attendance at a football game in
Las Vegas

"Most of my clichés aren't original."

Chuck Knox

"Trading quarterbacks is rare, but not unusual."

Joe Kuharich

"Concentration-wise, we're having trouble crossing the line mentally from a toughness standpoint."
Bill Parcells

"But I'm getting better since I took up that Sam Carnegie course."
Bill Petersen, on his
frequent malaprops

"Just remember the words of Henry Patrick—'kill me or let me live.'"
Bill Petersen

"The cliff dweller to end all cliff dwellers."
Bill Petersen, on an exciting game

"We're going to have a good time, but I don't want any of you players getting in trouble down there in Warsaw."
Bill Petersen, before his team traveled
to play in the Sun Bowl, just across
the border from Juarez, Mexico

"Don't you think for a minute that I'm going to take this loss standing down."
Bill Petersen

"Three things are bad for you. I can't remember the first two, but doughnuts are the third."
Bill Petersen

"They gave me a standing observation."
Bill Petersen

"I want to thank everyone who helped me get indicted."
Bill Petersen, on his induction into the Florida Hall of Fame

"I'm the football coach around here, and don't you remember it."
Bill Petersen, on his temper

"I want to gain fifteen hundred or two thousand yards, whichever comes first."
George Rogers

"I appreciate the condolences."
Curt Warner, congratulated on being picked third in the NFL draft

"He's like the Midas Muffler man. You can pay now or pay later."

> *Mark Clayton, on Dan Marino's*
> *five-year, $25-million contract*

"Normally, I sit down when the other team has the ball. Today, I stood on the sidelines. I kind of like to watch him work. I appreciate great performers."

> *Mike Webster, Steelers center, on*
> *watching Marino during a playoff*
> *game in which the Dolphins beat*
> *the Steelers*

HUGH McELHENNY

"That's the first time I ever touched him."

> *Don Paul, Rams linebacker, on*
> *shaking hands with the great Hugh*
> *McElhenny after his career was over*

"If you can figure him out, don't ask me. He has been a mystery since day one."

Roberta McMahon, to a reporter
asking questions about her son Jim

"To call him brash is like calling the Johnstown flood a leak, or the *Titanic* a collision."

Jim Murray, on McMahon

MEDIA WATCH

"We'd have 30 seconds of respectful silence and then continue with enthusiasm."

George Atkinson, on the reaction of
players and coaches if the press box
blew up

"No, something much simpler—journalism."

Tom Cousineau, asked by a
reporter if he majored in basket
weaving in college

"What's the difference between a three-week-old puppy and a sportswriter? In six weeks, the puppy stops whining."

Mike Ditka

"Well, if you've got to have a bomb, I guess that's the best place for it."

Tom Landry, on a bomb scare in the press box

"The poor kid's got a warped mind. He wants to be a sportswriter."

Bo Schembechler, on the ambitions of his 16-year-old son

"It was a brain transplant. I got a sportswriter's brain so I would be sure I had one that hadn't been used."

Norm Van Brocklin, on his brain surgery

"When I heard about it, I spent two hours trying to rent a submarine."

George Young, on agent Leigh Steinberg taking a group of writers for a boat ride before the Super Bowl

"The New York media and fans are becoming like Paris during the French Revolution. They need to see somebody go to the guillotine every day."

George Young, on a 2–3 start by the Giants

MEDIOCRITY

"The coach kept me in the game for morale purposes—I made the other players feel superior."

Bud Winters, on his short-lived football career at the University of California

MEMORIES

"I don't have one bad memory from my 13 seasons. I don't have any memory at all, for that matter."

Bubba Baker

"Waking up from all my operations."

Tim Foley, on his best memories from his playing days

"Dan and I had our ups and downs. Once we didn't speak for two weeks. I didn't think it was right to interrupt him."

Bob Costas, on Dan Dierdorf

"If Howard Cosell had breakfast and dinner with everybody he bragged about on *Monday Night Football*, he'd weigh 723 pounds."

Joe Garagiola

"It makes as much sense as a secretary going home and spending nights typing."

Walter Payton, asked if he watched Monday Night Football

MONEY

"We don't supply women, so it must be money."

Bum Phillips, asked if Dennis Winston was holding out for money

MONKEY BUSINESS

"It's like we lifted King Kong off our shoulders.
Now we've got Cheetah on our backs, and we can
handle Cheetah."

> *Patrick Allen, Oilers cornerback, on*
> *winning a game after an eight-game*
> *losing streak*

"If me and King Kong went into an alley, only
one of us would come out, and it wouldn't be
the monkey."

> *Lyle Alzado*

JOE MONTANA

"I don't know if he'll be there with us in the Hall
of Fame. Hell, they might have to build this boy
his own wing."

> *Sammy Baugh, on Joe Montana*

"Joe Montana is not human. I don't want to call him a god, but he's definitely somewhere in between."

Cris Collinsworth

"If every game was a Super Bowl, Joe Montana would be undefeated."

Randy Cross

"Somebody asked me if we were going to do something special. I said Joe already has a state named after him."

John Moreschi, mayor of Montana's hometown, in Pennsylvania

"I'm just an average Joe compared to him. He's the absolute best I've ever seen."

Joe Namath, on Montana

MUSCLES

"That is because I don't have one."

Fran Tarkenton, on never pulling a muscle during his long career

"Probably the Beatles' *White Album*."
> *Steve Largent, asked after all the*
> *records he's broken, the one he*
> *cherishes the most*

"I'd hate to be a person who just lived. You only have one chance in your life to be Mozart."
> *Ronnie Lott*

"I guess I was the only NFL coach who was stupid enough to go along with it."
> *Bum Phillips, on appearing in a*
> *music video with Boy George*

MYSTERIES

"I love guys who win them all."
> *LaVell Edwards, Brigham Young*
> *University coach, on why he loves*
> *Sherlock Holmes*

"When you hit him at the ankles, it was like getting an electric shock. If you hit him above the ankles, you were likely to get killed."

Red Grange, on Nagurski

"If you hit him low, he'd run over you. When you hit him high, he'd knock you down and run over you."

Mel Hein

"He was the only man I ever saw who ran his own interference."

Steve Owen

"Shoot him before he leaves the dressing room."

Steve Owen, on the best way to stop Nagurski

JOE NAMATH

"I spent 12 years training for a career that was over in a week. Joe Namath spent one week for a career that lasted 12 years."

> *Bruce Jenner, Olympic decathlon gold medalist*

"We didn't lose many games and we never lost a party."

> *Curley Johnson, Jets punter, on what it meant having Namath at quarterback*

NITTANY LIONS

"We have to play Penn State next year, so I really can't say SMU is better."

> *Foge Fazio, former Pittsburgh coach, asked who was better between the two teams that beat Pittsburgh— Penn State or SMU*

CHUCK NOLL

"His pedigree was super. He was by Paul Brown out of Sid Gillman by Don Shula."

> *Art Rooney, Steelers owner and*
> *racetrack owner, on how he*
> *knew Chuck Noll would make*
> *a great coach*

NOSE TO NOSE

"Looks like nobody guarded your nose."

> *Tim Krumrie, comments made*
> *to Bob Hope upon being introduced*
> *as noseguard on the AP*
> *All-American team*

NUMBERS GAME

"The guy in front of me got number 76 and the guy behind me got number 78."

> *Red Grange, on how he got the*
> *number 77*

"I look a lot faster when I wear 36."

Glenn Watson, Vanderbilt defensive
lineman, on changing his number
from 92 to 36

ODDS

"Who's the one guy who thinks we can do it?"

Mike Gottfried, Kansas coach, on
Kansas having odds of 100–1 of
winning the Big Eight title

OFF—SEASON

"I don't see anything to believe that he should
not work hard on football and not as hard on
his golf."

John McKay, on the off-season of
Buccaneers receiver Kevin House

OFF WEEK

"Rush Limbaugh is more likely to show up at a NOW conference."

> *Gary Plummer, 49ers player, asked if he was going to a Raiders game during the 49ers' off-week*

OFFENSE

"I thought 55 would have been enough."

> *Ed Farrell, Davidson coach, after losing a game to Furman, 63–55*

"I wasn't sure we'd ever get close enough to need it."

> *Lou Holtz, on why Arkansas wasn't practicing its goal-line offense*

"It's like saving up all your life to move out of a grubby tenement and then finding out you've moved next door."

> *Jim Cadile, on switching from center to guard after 11 years in the NFL*

"There would be a lot of offensive linemen playing indoor soccer next year."

> *Bob Golic, on what would happen had the 1987 ban on steroids been enforced*

"This time of year, if you're breathing, you're healthy."

> *Kent Hull, on playing on the offensive line late in the season*

"Show me an All-Pro offensive tackle and I'll show you a holder."

> *Henry Jordan*

"Hold when you're at home and don't hold when you're on the road."

> *John McKay, on his blocking strategy*

"If the meek are going to inherit the earth, our offensive linemen are going to be land barons."
Bill Muir, SMU coach

"It's not a position, it's a hideout. The only time they're asked for their autograph is on a checkout line at the supermarket."
Jim Murray, on the anonymity of offensive linemen

"I'm a 'Save the Whales' guy."
George Young, on why he likes offensive linemen

OFFICIALS

"Officials are the only guys who can rob you and then get a police escort out of the stadium."
Ron Bolton

"We have a motto that goes, 'To err is human. To forgive is against league policy.'"
Mark Duncan, former director of personnel for the NFL

"Players in the league, they don't play after age 40.
I think it should be the same for refs."

Todd Lyght

"I know why we lost the Civil War. We must have
had the same officials."

Bum Phillips, coach of the South,
after the North beat the South in the
Senior Bowl

"You have to be respectful when arguing with an
official. I usually say, 'Sir, are we watching the
same game?' "

Homer Smith, former
West Point coach

OILERS

"We were tipping off our plays. Whenever we broke
from the huddle, three backs were laughing and
one was pale as a ghost."

John Breen, former Oilers general
manager, on a very bad Oilers team

"If God tapped me on the shoulder and told me I had to play another season with the Oilers, I'd retire."

Cris Dishman

"I feel like I'm playing against two teams—our offense and their offense."

Cris Dishman, on a bad Oilers offensive team

"Can you imagine what would have happened if we'd won?"

Andy Dorris, on more than 40,000 fans welcoming home the Oilers after they lost to the Steelers in the 1979 conference championship game

"Being called untrustworthy by Bud Adams is like being called ugly by a bullfrog."

Bob Lanier, mayor of Houston, on Oilers owner Bud Adams claiming that the city of Houston did not negotiate with the team in good faith

OPENING DAY

"You're not going to win every game, but I hate to prove it right off the bat."

Jerry Burns, after losing his debut as Vikings coach

"Opening games make me nervous. To tell you the truth, I'd rather open with our second game."

John McKay

OPPOSITION

"I'm regarded as somewhat of an authority. If I build up another team, they're liable to believe it."

Woody Hayes, on why he never builds up Ohio State opponents

OWNERS

"The U.S. Congress can declare war with a simple majority, but we need a three-quarters majority to go to the john."

Art Modell, Ravens owner, on what it takes to change NFL rules

"We're 28 Republicans who vote Socialist."

Art Modell, on how he and the other owners share television money and gate receipts

PACKERS

"There are three important things in life: family, religion, and the Green Bay Packers."

Vince Lombardi

"If a contest had 97 prizes, the 98th would be a trip to Green Bay."

John McKay

"They overwhelmed one opponent, underwhelmed 10, and whelmed one."

Red Smith, on the Packers' 1958
record of 1–10–1

PAIN GAME

"Speed, strength, and the inability to register pain immediately."

Reggie Williams, on his
greatest strengths

PAPA BEAR

"I get along with Halas just fine. If he'd paid me a little more, I might have even liked him."
Doug Atkins, on George Halas

"He throws nickels around like manhole covers."
Mike Ditka, on the legendary
cheapness of George Halas

"I came cheap."

*George Halas, on why he took over
the Bears in 1933 after retiring as
player-coach in 1930*

"This is like Orville Wright coming back and
deciding to run United Airlines."

*Stan Jones, on George Halas deciding
to get more involved with the Bears
late in his career*

"Halas was famous for being associated with only
one club all his life—the one he held over your
head during salary talks."

*Bobby Layne, on negotiating
contracts with Halas*

PARTY ON

"All I know is that Richard Burton outlived
James Fixx."

*Sonny Jurgensen, on the virtues of a
wild lifestyle*

"If I'm sleeping, how will I know what kind of good time somebody is having without me?"

John Matuszak, on being told to go to sleep early the night before the Raiders were to play in the Super Bowl

"I'll stay out of bars when women cease to go in."

John Matuszak

"It's amateur night out there right now. I'll do my partying after. I've got five months."

Steve McMichael, on avoiding Bourbon Street before the Super Bowl

"There's nothing wrong with reading the game plan by the light of the jukebox."

Ken Stabler

PASSING GAME

"You have the option of catching it by either end."
*Johnny Unitas, on the wobbly passes
of Billy Kilmer*

JOE PATERNO

"Joe Paterno can coach until he's 100 years old and still beat these other guys [Big Ten coaches]."
Beano Cook

"Three out of four are guaranteed to go up the middle."
*Jeff Hostetler, on Joe Paterno
golf balls*

"Maybe I'll go home and ask for a raise."
*Joe Paterno, on passing Bear Bryant
to become the all-time winningest
bowl-game coach*

PENALTY

"No player is allowed to get a penalty unless he can get the yards back."

Lou Holtz, on his innovative
way of trying to have his team avoid
penalties

PETS

"I'm not a dog and I have my own house."

Richard Dent, on being in Mike
Ditka's doghouse

"Needless to say, people don't stop by very often."

Mosi Tatupu, on his four pet pit bulls

PLANES, TRAINS, AND AUTOMOBILES

"If you beat Houston, you go home by bus. If you lose, you have to fly back to New York."

> *Sammy Baugh, New York Titans*
> *coach, after a rough flight the team*
> *made to Houston*

"I tell people playing a football game feels like being in a three- or four-car wreck. And I ought to know, because I was in one last month."

> *Don Beebe*

"The good Lord might not want to take me, but He might be after the pilot."

> *Bobby Bowden, on his fear of*
> *small planes*

"I asked the pilot how we were doing. He said bad news and good news. The bad news was that we were lost. The good news was that we were making good time."

> *Bobby Bowden, on flying through*
> *a storm*

"You only have to bat a thousand in two things—flying and heart transplants. Everything else you can go four for five."

Beano Cook

"There are no films of irate customers to study."

Paul Jones, retired Seahawks wide receiver, on being a car salesman

"I didn't mind losing the second wife as much as losing the '56 Mercury to her. I loved that car. It was the first decent car I ever owned."

Big Daddy Lipscomb

"Sure, we're in limos—we're stars. How else is a star supposed to travel?"

Deion Sanders, on the Cowboys traveling around town in limos before Super Bowl XXX against the Steelers

PLAYBOOK

"I haven't seen a new play since I was in high school."

Red Grange (1971)

"It's the only time in my life that my wife let me buy the magazine."

>*Don James, Washington coach, on one*
>*of his players making the* Playboy
>*All-American team*

P L A Y O F F S

"We can't think about the playoffs. We would not even accept a bowl bid at this point in time."

>*Dan Henning, on his 5–6–1 record as*
>*Falcons coach*

"A game for losers played by losers."

>*Vince Lombardi, on the old*
>*runner-up bowl*

"That was three years ago. My attention span is about three minutes."

>*John Riggins, asked in 1984 if the*
>*Redskins' turnaround could be traced*
>*to a 1981 loss to the 49ers*

"One week you feel euphoric, the next you feel like a piece of slime on the bottom of the ocean."

> *Ron Wolf, Packers general manager,*
> *on beating the 49ers in one round of*
> *the playoffs and then losing to the*
> *Cowboys in the next round*

POLITICS

"If the FBI went far enough, I was always suspect. I never liked football."

> *Father Daniel Berrigan, on being*
> *released from prison during the*
> *Vietnam riots*

"Pro football gave me a great sense of perspective to enter politics. I'd already been booed, cheered, cut, sold, traded, and hung in effigy."

> *Jack Kemp*

"They're in a high enough income-tax bracket where most of them start thinking Republican."

> *Jeff Kemp, on getting some of his*
> *Seahawks teammates to volunteer for*
> *his dad's presidential campaign*

"Politics is an astonishing profession. It has enabled me to go from being an obscure member of the junior varsity at Harvard to becoming an honorary member of the Football Hall of Fame."
John F. Kennedy

"Being in politics is like being a football coach. You have to be smart enough to know the game and stupid enough to think it is important."
Eugene McCarthy

"I didn't vote for you, but you do have a nice suit on."

Don Meredith, during a visit by former Vice President Spiro Agnew to the Monday Night Football *booth*

"In life, as in a football game, the principle to follow is: Hit the line hard; don't foul and don't shirk, but hit the line hard."
Teddy Roosevelt

"It's a lot tougher to be a football coach than a president. You've got four years as president and they guard you. A coach doesn't have anyone to protect him when things go wrong."
Harry Truman

171

POLLS

"I told them the only way they could lose credibility quicker would be to put me in a swimsuit issue."

Lou Holtz, on Sports Illustrated's *preseason poll that had a bad Notre Dame team rated in the Top 20*

POVERTY

"I don't say my folks were poor, but when my uncle used to slice the ham at dinner, it had only one side."

Walt Garrison

"I was so poor, I had a tumbleweed as a pet."

Darrell Royal, on growing up

PRACTICE
MAKES PERFECT

"The one place at Michigan State I never was late to was practice. It didn't start until I got there."
Duffy Daugherty

"I'm so low, I could wear a top hat and crawl under the belly of a snake."
Walt Garrison, on a brutal practice

"It's shattering when a player loses interest in camp. When you lose your desire to stand around and eat steaks, you lose everything."
John McKay

"I don't think he's got much of a future here, because I plan on going to all the games."
John McKay, on placekicker Pete Rajecki having a bad camp with the Buccaneers because McKay made him nervous

"If I prepared for a concert the way I prepared for a football game, I would begin by throwing the piano out the window."

Mike Reid, on preparing for a
piano concert

PREVENT DEFENSE

"It is designed to prevent the other team from beating you with a bomb, so that they may march down the field and beat you with a field goal."

Tex Schramm, on the prevent defense

PRISON

"Three guys asked me to show them how to run out for a 250-yard pass."

Mark Gastineau, on a football clinic
he held at Riker's Island Prison

PRO BOWL

"If my life was based around the Pro Bowl, I'd be in trouble."

Irving Fryar, on not making the '96
Pro Bowl team despite a stellar year

"You go to the Pro Bowl and people looking at your T-shirt ask you what your average is. They think you're part of the pro bowlers' tour."

R. C. Thielemann, Redskins guard,
on making the Pro Bowl

PRO WRESTLING

"Wrestling is much tougher. Every night you have to drive a lot of miles to another arena."

Leo Nomellini, football great,
comparing his pro football career
to his pro wrestling career

PSYCHIC NETWORK

"How should I know? I'm Deion Sanders, not Dionne Warwick."

>*Deion Sanders, asked where he'll play in the future*

PSYCHOLOGY

"I've always considered myself a group therapist for 60,000 people. Every Sunday I held group therapy and the people came out to take out their frustrations on me."

>*Sonny Jurgensen*

PUNT RETURNS

"It's like embalming. Nobody likes it, but someone has to do it."

>*Greg Pruitt, on being a punt-return specialist*

"I felt like a deer with a hundred hunters after me."

> *Deion Sanders, after returning a punt for a touchdown*

PUNTING

"Anything that goes up that high and travels that far ought to have a stewardess on it."

> *Sam DeLuca, on a Ray Guy punt*

"I kicked six days a week and took Sunday off—just like I did last season."

> *Dave Jennings, on his training-camp routine following a lousy season*

"I am the oratorical equivalent of a blocked punt."

> *Tommy Prothro, on his public-speaking skills*

"When in doubt, punt."
Knute Rockne

"I figured I was kicking against the air-conditioning."
Bill Van Heusen, punter, after a lousy kick in the Superdome

"It's a shankless job."
Bryan Wagner, after punting the ball 91 times in one season

QUARTERBACKS

"If you studied to be a lawyer but couldn't pass the bar exam, would you become a bailiff just to stay in the courtroom?"
Gary Beban, on quitting pro football rather than changing from the quarterback position

"To hell with the quarterbacks. They don't care about me if I get hurt."

Richard Dent, defensive lineman, on having no sympathy for a series of quarterback injuries

"Most of them look like they belong in Malibu."

Art Donovan, on the current crop of quarterback pretty boys

"He proves it every day in practice by over-throwing receivers."

Hayden Fry, Iowa coach, on Mark Vlasic's comment that he has a better arm than starting quarterback Chuck Long

"The way to succeed at quarterback is to call the unexpected consistently."

John Hadl

"Having a pro offense with great receivers but no first-rate quarterback is like having a new limousine with a chimpanzee at the wheel."

Charlie Tate, former University of Miami coach

"It's amazing what the human body can do when chased by a bigger human body."

> *Jack Thompson, quarterback, on running for 10 touchdowns at Washington State*

"A quarterback doesn't come into his own until he can tell the coach to go to hell."

> *Johnny Unitas*

"They ought to be good. They play more golf than we do."

> *Fuzzy Zoeller, golf pro, on several NFL quarterbacks getting birdies at a tournament*

QUITTING TIME

"I knew it was time to quit when I was chewing out an official and he walked off the penalty faster than I could keep up with him."

> *George Halas*

RADIO

"Max McGee had the perfect face for radio."
> *Paul Hornung, poking fun at his*
> *good friend*

"I know Troy is always talking to somebody out there, and they may be talking about me."
> *Nate Newton, on why he did not*
> *want a radio in his helmet like the*
> *one Troy Aikman has*

RAIDERS

"It's kind of like watching your wife eat dinner at somebody else's house."
> *Howie Long, on the first time he*
> *played against longtime Raiders*
> *teammate Marcus Allen*

"He's a good coach, a good tactician, but not a leader. He's like cold dishwater."
> *John Matuszak, on Raiders coach*
> *Tom Flores*

"If you would turn them over to us, we'd put them in silos, and we wouldn't have to build the MX missile."

Ronald Reagan, on the Raiders

"We were the only team in pro football whose team picture showed both a front and side view."

Ken Stabler, on the Raiders'
outlaw image

"I don't blame them. Los Angeles probably would steal their athletes just like they stole our Raiders."

Pete Stark, congressman from
Oakland, on the Soviet boycott
of the 1984 summer Olympics in
Los Angeles

RAMBLIN' MAN

"I've got the kind of furniture that when you snap your fingers, it jumps into the crate."

Jerry Glanville, on the many moves
he's made over his 20 years of
coaching

"My kids think Atlas Van Lines is the school bus."
Pepper Rodgers, on his many team
changes as a football coach

R A M S

"The people of St. Louis will be all excited to get this team. And then they'll realize Georgia Frontiere is still the owner."
Roman Gabriel, on the Rams moving
to St. Louis

"If the Rams don't choke, I'll choke them."
Thomas Henderson, on the Cowboys
playing the Rams in the 1979 NFC
title game

"One day you don't even have a team, and the next day you're in last place."
Jay Leno, on St. Louis getting
the Rams

"It's just like you're riding down the road, you get your car washed, and boom—all of a sudden it starts raining."

Leslie O'Neal, on the 2–7 record of
the Rams

RAZORBACKS

"Fayetteville isn't the end of the world, but you can see it from there."

Lou Holtz, on the University of
Arkansas campus at Fayetteville

RECORDS

"Our record is 4–3 and 2. It sounds like the combination to a lock."

Dick Tomey, former Arizona coach

RECRUITMENT

"The only thing I know for sure is that the
linemen are ugly and the receivers are pretty."
*George MacIntyre, Vanderbilt coach,
on evaluating recruits*

"OU is easier to spell than OSU."
*Barry Switzer, on why Oklahoma
has an advantage in recruiting over
Oklahoma State University*

REDSKINS

"If the rest of Washington ran as efficiently as this
football team, there wouldn't be any deficit."
*Jeff Bostic, on the glory days of
the Redskins*

RELATIONSHIPS

"We have a strange and wonderful relationship: he's strange and I'm wonderful."

Mike Ditka, on his relationship with
Jim McMahon

"We never talked when I was in Chicago."

Buddy Ryan, asked if he and Mike
Ditka had talked after Ryan left the
Bears' staff to coach the Eagles

RELIGION

"You want to know what a real test of faith is? That's when you go to church and reach into your pocket and all you got is a $20 bill."

Bobby Bowden

"God is always on the side which has the best football coach."

Heywood Hale Broun

"I called up dial-a-prayer and they hung up on me."
Mack Brown, Tulane coach, after his team lost its first seven games

"No, we've got so many things to pray for, we'd get penalized 15 yards for delaying the start of the game."
Fred Casoti, Colorado assistant athletic director, when asked if his football team had any pregame prayers

"All those college football coaches who hold dressing-room prayers before a game should be forced to attend church once a week."
Duffy Daugherty

"The good Lord has more to do than worry about the outcome of a football game."
Duffy Daugherty, on religion and football

"An atheist is a guy who watches a Notre Dame–SMU football game and doesn't care who wins."
Dwight Eisenhower

"More than being concerned with who's going to win the Super Bowl, I feel the Lord is probably more concerned that they might find a day other than Sunday to play it on."

Billy Graham

"The good Lord allows just so much profanity on a team, and I use up our entire quota."

Lou Holtz

"God's busy. They'll have to make do with me."

John McKay, asked if his team prayed for victory

"When it comes to football, God is prejudiced toward big, fast kids."

Chuck Mills, Wake Forest coach

"I find that prayers work best when you have big players."

Knute Rockne

RESTAURANT ROW

"He's tougher than a Waffle House steak."
Jerry Glanville, on Saints
quarterback Bobby Hebert

RETIREMENT AGE

"My wife and family are very pleased. They all forgot I had a good disposition."
Frank Broyles, on retiring as
Arkansas football coach

"The thing that really sealed it was getting chosen to play in an old-timers' game and I hadn't even retired yet."
Ruben Carter

"I'm not a boxer. I'm only going to do this once."
Randy Cross, on his retirement from
the NFL

"When nobody showed up, I said the heck with it and decided to play another year."

> *John Fitzgerald, Cowboys center, on*
> *announcing his retirement*

"It's time I got my golf game back in shape."

> *Otto Graham, on retiring as*
> *athletic director of the U.S.*
> *Coast Guard Academy*

"At the moment, I'm unemployed. If anybody knows of anything out there that pays $300,000 a year . . ."

> *Tom Jackson, on his retirement*

"When I retired, nobody even came with a Brownie camera."

> *John Niland, upon hearing that more*
> *than two hundred reporters covered*
> *Roger Staubach's announcement*

"I ain't doing a damn thing, and I don't start until noon."

> *Bum Phillips, on his retirement*

"Mine is the only jersey retired while I was playing."

Steve Raible, Seahawks wide receiver

JERRY RICE

"Jerry Rice has more touchdowns than NASA."
Roy Firestone

"Double coverage and prayers. He's the best I've ever seen."

Everson Walls, on what it takes to stop Jerry Rice

"I think he believes that if they covered him with eleven guys, he should still be open and win the game."

Steve Young, on Rice

JOHN RIGGINS

"On game days, John tells us, 'Hey, just get the wagon out, hitch it up, and I'll pull it. Everybody get on.'"

Joe Gibbs, on workhorse John Riggins

"I have a penchant for the bizarre. I don't like to believe everybody else. I don't know if I'm ahead or behind . . . but I know I'm not even."

John Riggins

RIVALRIES

"We'll dominate them physically, mentally, and then we'll steal their girlfriends."

Steve Martin, center at Cal State–Northridge, on his team's rivalry with Cal State–Hayward

ROAD GAMES

"I play as well on the road as I do at home, but my teams don't."

Lou Holtz, on why he hates road games

ROOKIES

"People expect too much from rookies; rookies don't expect enough of themselves."
Marv Levy

"All the rookies call me Mr. Long and I can't recognize any of the music they listen to."

Howie Long, asked how he knew his career was almost over

ROYALTY

"Steve has the Midas touch—everything he touches turns to mufflers."

> *Jim Walden, Washington State coach, on Steve Raible*

PETE ROZELLE

"If Pete Rozelle had been in charge during World War II, Germany and Japan would still be in the running and Ethiopia would have been a wild-card finalist."

> *Gordon Beard, sportswriter, on Pete Rozelle's implementation of an expanded playoffs*

"If Richard Nixon had Pete Rozelle's publicity staff, he still would be president."

> *Al Davis*

"He always knew how to operate in that jungle. I know the jungle. I came out of it."

Art Modell, on Pete Rozelle's genius for marketing

"As a PR man, he is without equal. He could have made Castro president of the United States."

Jim Murray

RULES

"There will be no fighting in barrooms, unless the head coach is pinned down, in which case he should be rescued."

Jerry Glanville, on the team rules he imposed as coach

RUNNING BACKS

"Thirty is a grandpa for a running back in the NFL."

Walt Garrison

"No one ever taught me, and I can't teach anyone."
Red Grange

"You want to punish the running backs. You like to kick them and when they sit down, kick them again—until they wave the white flag."
Greg Lloyd

"A good back makes his own holes. Anyone can run where the holes are."
Joe Don Looney

"If you needed four yards, you'd give the ball to Garrison and he'd get you four yards. If you needed 20 yards, you'd give the ball to Garrison and he'd get you four yards."
Don Meredith, on Walt Garrison

"Each time it's like being in a head-on car accident."
Matt Snell, on carrying the ball in the NFL

"Sometimes it's like being in the mountains, maybe like Jamaica, but then there's sunlight streaming down a narrow line and you stop following the mountains and just follow the sunlight."

Duane Thomas, on open-field running

BUDDY RYAN

"Buddy was like my favorite uncle. The one I wanted to tell, 'Shut up.'"

Gary Fencik

"I think with me what you see is what you get. But some people don't like what they see."

Buddy Ryan

SACK ATTACK

"A product of uncontrolled rage."
Lyle Alzado, defining a sack

"By the fourth quarter, I was out of breath. I almost called time out, just so I could go over and rest."
Chris Chandler, on being sacked
seven times in a game

"When I get a sack, it really fires me up to get another. I guess I get myself into a sadistic state of mind."
Fred Cook, Colts lineman

SALARY

"I figured I could survive with a half-million dollars until March 1995."
Antonio Langhan, on his rookie
season in which he had his salary
deferred until the 1994–95 season

SALESMAN

"She was wrong. By the end of the season, I'd sold our stereo, our car, her jewels, and our television."

Lou Holtz, on his part-time job selling cemetery plots early in his career, even though his wife told him he couldn't sell anything

BARRY SANDERS

"It's like a pinball machine. He's the ball, and everybody else is the post."

Dan Henning, on Barry Sanders

"He makes you miss so bad, you kind of look up in the stands and wonder if anybody's looking at you."

D. J. Johnson

"I've never seen anyone break so many tackles. We thought he had silicone on his pants, the way we kept slipping off him."

Keith Millard

DEION SANDERS

"He . . . ceases to amaze me."

> *Sid Bream, on Sanders's pursuit of*
> *careers in both baseball and football*

GALE SAYERS

"He looks no different than any other runner
when he's coming at you, but when he gets there,
he's gone."

> *George Donnelly, 49ers defensive*
> *back, on trying to tackle Sayers*

"I just wonder how many Sayers would have scored
if we hadn't set our defense to stop him."

> *Y. A. Tittle, 49ers assistant coach, on*
> *Sayers's six touchdowns in one game*
> *against them*

SCALPING

"The only difference between me and General
Custer is that I had to watch the films on Sunday."
Rick Venturi, former Northwestern
coach, on losing to Ohio State by the
score of 63–20

SCANDALS

"Everybody loves a good joke. That's why we have
pet rocks and in-house investigations by colleges."
Blackie Sherrod, on
scandals in college football's
Southwest Conference

SCHEDULE

"We don't have to beat North Dakota and Wichita
and Drake to wonder if we can play football. We'll
play Notre Dame and find out right away."
Bo Schembechler, on Michigan's
tough schedule

SCHOOL DAZE

"It didn't bother me that I ranked 234th in my high school graduating class of 273—until I heard the principal say it was a stupid class."

Lou Holtz

SCRAMBLIN' MAN

"I'm not particularly interested in scrambling and creating, because that's where you create interceptions, that's where you create problems. We don't want jazz musicians. We want classical musicians."

Chuck Noll

"If my quarterback runs, I'll shoot him."

Bill Parcells, defining a run-and-shoot offense

"Give your outside linebackers hand grenades."

Sam Rutigliano, on the best way to stop Jim Zorn from scrambling

"That's one rush Jim Plunkett could avoid."

Gary Shandling, on a story about
lava from a volcano traveling at a
rate of three feet per hour

"The only running I do is from sideline to huddle and from huddle to sideline. Anything beyond that would get us penalized for delay of game."

Norm Snead, slow-footed quarterback

"You have to know when and how to go down. The key is to have a fervent desire to be in on the next play."

Jim Zorn, on being a
running quarterback

SECOND STRING

"It's kind of difficult to introduce a guy you hope gets the flu every week."

Gary Hogeboom, Cowboys backup
quarterback, introducing starting
quarterback Danny White at a roast

"He has to be smart to get paid that much for carrying a clipboard."

> *Steve Nelson, on why he considers*
> *Don Strock, Dan Marino's longtime*
> *backup, as one of the NFL's smartest*
> *quarterbacks*

"I've graduated from clipboard to headset."

> *Cliff Stoudt, on moving from the*
> *Steelers' number-three quarterback to*
> *their number-two quarterback*

"I don't think I've been asked this many questions since my mother caught me drinking in high school."

> *Don Strock, facing the media after*
> *replacing Dan Marino in a game*

SECONDARY

"I treat pass receivers the way you would treat a burglar in your home."

> *George Atkinson, on his role in the*
> *Raiders' secondary*

"Do we have to start at one?"

> *Tom Landry, asked to rate the*
> *Cowboys' secondary on a scale of*
> *one to ten*

"Playing cornerback is like being on an island—
people can see you but they can't help you."
> *Eddie Lewis*

SEMIPROS

"We didn't have a team bus. We had a team bike."

> *Johnny Unitas, on his days in*
> *semipro ball*

SEX

"They're married to them."

> *Forrest Gregg, asked why he let the*
> *Bengals players sleep with their wives*
> *before the Super Bowl*

"I can remember the old days when sex was dirty and the air was clean."
Woody Hayes

"I love football. I really love football. As far as I'm concerned, it's the second-best thing in the world."
Joe Namath

"Either I don't know how to watch films or you don't know how to make love."
Bum Phillips, after Sid Gillman said that watching game films was more fun than making love

DON SHULA

"Describing Don Shula as intense is like describing the universe as fairly large."
Dave Barry

"If a nuclear bomb is dropped on this country, the only thing I'm sure will survive will be AstroTurf and Don Shula."
Bubba Smith

SHUTOUT

"Much ado about nothing to nothing."

> *Tim Cohane, on Pittsburgh's third*
> *straight scoreless tie, against*
> *Fordham in 1937*

SMALLTOWN, USA

"It's a very small town. It's so small, in fact, that the number-one industry there is taking bottles back to the store."

> *Monte Clark, on his hometown of*
> *Kingsburg, California*

BRUCE SMITH

"Bruce's target is the ball. Carry it at your peril. It is as if he is a bear and you have one of his cubs in your hand."

> *Jim Murray, on Bruce Smith*

EMMITT SMITH

"Give that little man just a crease and he's something special. He can stop on a dime and give you nine and a half cents change."
Nate Newton, on Emmitt Smith

SNAKE

"Eight beers and two hours' sleep a night."
Pete Banaszak, on Ken Stabler's training style

"In the NFL, there are 25 guys who can throw better than I can. But I can make guys win."
Ken Stabler

SONNY

"If we'd had you in Green Bay, we never would have lost."
Vince Lombardi, to Sonny Jurgensen

SOONERS

"We like to run and nobody likes to pass."
> *Billy Tubbs, former Oklahoma*
> *basketball coach, on why the*
> *Oklahoma basketball team was*
> *similar to the football team*

SPARTANS

"Me."
> *Duffy Daugherty, asked whom he*
> *was happiest to see returning to*
> *Michigan State*

SPEED RACER

"Any person in the field can catch me from behind.
That includes the officials."
> *Fred Biletnikoff, Hall of Fame*
> *wide receiver*

"I got tired of running down the field and having the ball land 30 yards behind me."

Greg Foster, world-champion hurdler,
on why he gave up trying to be a
wide receiver

"Maybe I've lost a step, but I had a few to lose."
Roy Green, on turning 34

"I knew he was fast, but I never knew how fast until I saw him playing tennis by himself."
Lou Holtz, on Rocket Ismail

"When I started out, I looked like Barry Sanders, and when I finished I looked like Colonel Sanders."

Reggie Johnson, 250-pound tight
end, on running back a kickoff
35 yards

"He creates a draft when he goes by."
George Perles, on the speed of
Tim Brown

"He's quick as a hiccup."
Jim Wacker, Minnesota coach, on
quarterback Marquel Fleetwood

"He has two speeds—here he comes and there he goes."

Barry Wilborn, on Roy Green

SPRING PRACTICE

"I never really believed in spring practice. It doesn't tell you anything. It was like having your daughter coming in at four o'clock in the morning with a Gideon Bible."

Duffy Daugherty

"It was about normal—no worse than an ordinary death march."

Lou Holtz, on spring practice

"The only reason I played baseball at all in college was to get out of spring football."

Tom Paciorek, on being a college linebacker before his days as a professional baseball player

"If spring practice created revenues there would be no cutbacks."

> *Barry Switzer, on cutbacks in spring practices at Oklahoma*

STAMP COLLECTING

"At Arkansas, they made a stamp to commemorate you; then, after last year, they had to stop making it because people were spitting on the wrong side."

> *Lou Holtz, on a tough year at Arkansas*

BART STARR

"We hitched our wagon to a Starr."

> *Jim Taylor, crediting the greatness of the Packers to Bart Starr*

STATS

"Statistics always remind me of the fellow who drowned in a river whose average depth was only three feet."

Woody Hayes

"Statistics and records are baseball talk. They keep records like most times sliding into second base on a Tuesday."

John McKay

STEELERS

"If pro football ever dies out, and historians want to show what a player looked like when the game was at its peak, they could do worse than bury a Pittsburgh Steeler."

Ray Fitzgerald

"People are ranking us up there with the fabled Packers and Dolphins. It's nice to be fabled."

Ray Mansfield, on the Steelers' dynasty years

"With so many Super Bowl rings, maybe they'll all retire and go into the jewelry business."
John McKay

"Injuries kill you. I remember in Pittsburgh, we had no players and the ones we did have wanted to stay at the hotel by the fire. I was ticked because that's where I wanted to stand."
John McKay, on the Buccaneers
losing 42–0 to the Steelers

"We consider our Super Bowl trophy an antique."
Chuck Noll, on Opening Day,
after winning the Super Bowl
the year before

"Nope, but it would be if we get there after a Saturday-night game."
Bum Phillips, asked if it helped the
Oilers that the Steelers play them on
a Sunday after playing on the
previous Monday

"They can put on my tombstone: 'He'd 'a' lasted a lot longer if he hadn't played Pittsburgh six times in two years.'"
Bum Phillips

"The harder we played, the behinder we got."
Bum Phillips, on the Oilers losing to
Pittsburgh in the playoffs, 34–5

KORDELL STEWART

"He's the best thing to happen to Pittsburgh since U.S. Steel."
Jim Murray, on Kordell Stewart

STORMY WEATHER

"Any kid who would leave that wonderful weather is too dumb to play for us."
Alex Agase, Purdue football coach,
on not recruiting in California

"It was so muddy, people planted rice at halftime."
Tony Demeo, Mercyhurst coach, on a
game played on a muddy field

"I'd have played it in the ocean if I had to, and I can't even swim."

> *L. C. Greenwood, on bad weather in an AFC championship game*

"Since I've been at Minnesota there have been three weather reports on recruiting weekends—bitterly cold, unbearably cold, and unbelievably cold."

> *Lou Holtz*

"It was so muddy that when I went to congratulate the Carolina players, I discovered they were mine."

> *Tom Nugent, former Maryland football coach, on losing in the rain to North Carolina*

"What do you think I am—a geologist?"

> *Bill Petersen, asked if he thought it might rain before a game*

"You can't practice being miserable."

> *Bum Phillips, asked if the Oilers were properly prepared for a game they lost to the Browns in subzero weather*

"The only elements that affected us were the 11 wearing red jerseys."

> *Bum Phillips, on the Saints losing*
> *35–0 to the Falcons in windy,*
> *rainy weather*

STRIKE OUT

"It was like making up my mind about who I hated most in World War II—Japan or Germany."

> *Beano Cook, on choosing sides in the*
> *baseball strike*

"It's kind of like coaching an All-Star team without all-stars."

> *John Robinson, on coaching scabs*
> *during the football strike*

"We might have the worst bunch of guys together we've ever seen as a football team. I don't know what anybody else has, but I'd trade mine with anybody, sight unseen."

> *Buddy Ryan, Eagles coach, on his*
> *replacement team getting murdered*
> *by the Bears' replacement team*

"Our game plan is for our coaches to learn everybody's name."

Al Saunders, Chargers coach, on coaching during the football strike

"Put it this way. If Richard Burton got sick the night before playing Macbeth in New York, he wouldn't be worried if Pee Wee Herman replaced him for a day."

Billy Ray Smith, on concerns about replacement players taking over for regulars during the football strike

STRONGMEN

"If we win a big game, I like my players to be strong enough to carry me off the field."

Lou Holtz, on the significance he places on physical strength

SUPER BOWL

"Losing the Super Bowl is worse than death. You have to get up the next morning."
George Allen

"I don't like it. Now I have to pay taxes in three states."
Buddy Bell, Chiefs linebacker and resident of Minnesota, on Super Bowl I being held at a neutral site

"The Super Bowl has become Main Street's Mardi Gras."
Norman Chad

"I feel like some guy who picked up a Rubik's Cube and got it right the first time."
Cris Collinsworth, on playing in the Super Bowl in his rookie year

"I feel like a rat in a cheese factory with the cat on vacation."
Thomas "Hollywood" Henderson, on the Cowboys playing in the Super Bowl

"My high school team never turned it over nine times."

> *Kent Hull, Bills lineman, on the Bills' losing Super Bowl 52–17 with nine turnovers*

"You know, greed will set in, and say, 'maybe we can win two.'"

> *Keith Jackson, asked if he would retire if the Packers won Super Bowl XXXI*

"After that game, we could have played the Girl Scouts and we wouldn't have taken it as a joke."

> *John Mackey, after the Colts lost to the Jets in Super Bowl III*

"We'd be two wins away from the Super Bowl if we were playing in the NFL."

> *Doug MacLean, Florida Panthers hockey coach, on the team's 13–5 start to the 1995–96 season*

"I felt like one of the losers at Pompeii."

> *Curtis McClinton, on the Chiefs losing Super Bowl I to the Packers*

"The question is: Is Bourbon Street ready for me?"

Jim McMahon, on being asked before
Super Bowl XX in New Orleans if he
was ready for Bourbon Street

"I'd run over Grimm's mother, too."

Matt Millen, Raiders linebacker, after
Redskins offensive lineman Russ
Grimm said he would run over his
own mother to win Super Bowl XVII

"You're only great if you win something. Alexander wasn't Alexander the Mediocre or Alexander the Average. He was Alexander the Great, and there's a reason for it."

Sterling Sharpe, on the significance
of winning the Super Bowl

SUPERSTITIONS

"I don't like to jump from tall buildings before big games."

John Campana, Bucknell guard,
asked if he had any superstitions

SUSPENSIONS

"We've got two rookie guards who slept a lot better last night than the night or two before."

> *Joe Woolley, Cardinals executive, on*
> *Leon Lett being suspended just*
> *before the Cardinals were to face*
> *the Cowboys*

SWEET SCIENCE

"He's the best defensive end in football, and the worst fighter I ever saw."

> *Thomas Henderson, on the short-lived*
> *boxing career of Ed "Too Tall" Jones*

"I have never been around so many crummy people in all my days."

> *Ed "Too Tall" Jones, on his*
> *boxing career*

"Maybe those guys who carried messages city to city covered more yardage. You know, the guys in Greece. But as far as we know, Payton's the greatest."

Darryl Grant, on Walter Payton

"I said to them, 'All right, you guys, don't tackle him for a loss on the next play and make us go through all of this again.'"

Jay Hilgenberg, Bears center, said to the Saints on the play after Payton broke Jim Brown's rushing record

"I'm holding out for a card on Trivial Pursuit. My agent and I are waiting to negotiate."

Jim Kovach, on tackling Payton after he broke Brown's rushing record

"You felt honored to tackle him."

Matt Millen, on Payton

"When God created a running back, he created Walter Payton."

Johnny Roland

"I'm a hell of a lot more worried about a guy named Walter Payton."

> *Randy White, asked if the Cowboys*
> *were concerned about tackling*
> *William "Refrigerator" Perry*

TALK TOO MUCH

"The best way to save face is by keeping the lower part of it shut."

> *Lou Holtz*

"When all is said and done, as a rule, more is said than done."

> *Lou Holtz*

FRAN TARKENTON

"I haven't hit him yet, and now I never will."

> *Doug Buffone, on the retirement of*
> *Fran Tarkenton, one of football's*
> *all-time great scramblers*

LAWRENCE TAYLOR

"Everybody knows he's coming. It's like a cop putting sirens on his car."

Beasley Reece, on Lawrence Taylor

TEEN YEARS

"Naw, it wasn't a gang. It was a group of felons having fun."

Ickey Woods, on hanging out with a gang when he was growing up

TEMPER, TEMPER

"Because John McEnroe never played it."

Larry Felser, sports columnist, on why so many millions of people love pro football

"I like my boys to be agile, mobile, and hostile."
Jake Gaither, longtime coach of
Florida A & M

TERRAPINS

"The University of Maryland football team members all made straight As. Their Bs are a little crooked."
Johnny Walker, Baltimore disk jockey

TEXAS

"Living in a small town in Texas ain't half bad—if you own it."
Bobby Layne, on Lubbock, Texas

"Since the fuel shortage, we Texans are wearing two-gallon hats."
Bobby Layne

"I talked to him briefly on the phone for an hour and a half."

Tony Kornheiser, on Joe Theismann's propensity for talking

"You leave a light on in the bathroom and he'd do twenty minutes to an empty shower."
Tony Kornheiser

"If talking was an Olympic sport, Theismann is Jim Thorpe."
Mike Lupica

THINKING MAN'S GAME

"You draw Xs and Os on a blackboard and that's not so difficult. I can even do it with my left hand."

John McKay, on the difficulty of football

"Every time you make a football player think, you're handicappin' him."
Bum Phillips

"Paralysis by analysis."
Tommy Prothro, on overanalyzing the Xs and Os of football

"When I went to Catholic high school in Philadelphia, we just had one coach for football and basketball. He took all of us who turned out and had us run through a forest. The ones who ran into the trees were on the football team."
George Raveling

THIRD AND LONG

"Wade is the man we'll turn to when it's third and a quarter-mile to go."
Donnie Duncan, former Iowa State coach, on Michael Wade, a wide receiver who was a quarter-mile champion in high school

"When it's third and long, you can take the milk drinkers and I'll take the whiskey drinkers every time."

Max McGee

THURMAN THOMAS

"It's like he runs with snow tires and everybody else on the field has sneakers."

Dave Adolph, on Thurman Thomas

TIES

"I don't know how to feel. I'll have to go kiss my sister and see which is better."

Scott Campbell, Purdue quarterback,
after a 29–29 tie

TIME OF POSSESSION

"Time of possession only counts in jail."
Pat Haden

"The only important thing about time of
possession is who gets to keep the ball after
the game is over."
Lou Holtz

TOOTH DECAY

"It's all word of mouth."
*Bill Lenkaitis, Patriots center and a
dentist, on building up his practice*

"I'm not going to eat any frogs or swallow
any worms, if that's what you mean. My wife's
a dentist. She wouldn't let me. Well, only if
I flossed."
*Glen Mason, Kansas coach, on his
willingness to do almost anything to
beat rival Kansas State*

"I didn't know how to react. I looked over the line of scrimmage and there was a guy with teeth."
> *Derland Moore, defensive lineman,*
> *on facing Joe Pellegrini instead of*
> *ten-year veteran Jeff Van Note, who*
> *was injured before the game*

TOUCHDOWNS

"It's the one where the player pitches the ball back to the official after scoring a touchdown."
> *Bear Bryant, asked to describe his*
> *favorite play*

"I was thinking I had just crossed the goal line."
> *Roger Craig, asked what his*
> *thoughts were after scoring his*
> *third touchdown in Super Bowl XIX*

"We never had to practice kicking off."
> *Tunch Ilkin, on the advantages of the*
> *Steelers not scoring many touchdowns*

TRADE WINDS

"It looks like they run and jump and do everything football players do."

Dave Casper, his reaction about being traded to the Oilers from the Raiders

"Religiously speaking, it's an advancement from a Cardinal to a Saint."

Conrad Dobler, on being traded from the St. Louis Cardinals to the New Orleans Saints

TROUBLEMAKERS

"Sometimes you had to pick up an ornery cuss you'd never want to hold the end of your rope, instead of some good ol' boy who'd get you beat 21–7."

Bum Phillips, on the role of troublemakers on a team

TURNOVERS

"You'd think that those are things we could work on and overcome. We've worked on them and perfected them."

> *Darryl Rogers, former Lions coach,*
> *on the Lions' continuing to turn over*
> *the ball despite hours of practice*

"Turnovers are like ex-wives. The more you have, the more they cost you."

> *Dave Widell, Cowboys lineman*

TWO-POINT CONVERSIONS

"I told my players, 'Watch the fake' and that's what they did. They watched the fake."

> *John Durham, Keystone Oaks High*
> *School coach, on losing a game on a*
> *two-point conversion*

"I'm not sure it's even David versus Goliath. It's more like David versus Goliath's big brother."

Jim Hofner, Cornell coach, on
playing Stanford

"Underdog, overdog, hotdog. I guess you want to be an underdog—but an underdog with the best team."

John McKay, on the Buccaneers
being an underdog in a playoff game

"You gotta practice. David went out there and practiced—slinging those rocks and tin cans and old beer bottles for days."

Bill Petersen, on David and Goliath

"I think we had the courage of David. We just didn't have the skills of David."

Lou Tepper, Illinois coach, on
reading his team the story of David
and Goliath before losing to Ohio
State, 48–6

UNIFORMS

"The reason women don't play football is because 11 of them would never wear the same outfit in public."
Phyllis Diller

"I think all uniforms look nice if you've got good players in 'em."
Bill Parcells, on uniform designs

UPSETS

"A blind hog finds an acorn if he keeps rooting."
Hayden Fry, Iowa coach, on upset wins over Nebraska and UCLA

"It's like getting up in the morning and reading the obituary column. You're glad you're not in it."
Lou Holtz, on Notre Dame not being one of several ranked teams upset in college football

"When I took this job I promised our fans I'd show them a Rose Bowl team."

> *Lee Corso, Indiana coach, on putting*
> *USC on their schedule*

"I sell cactus. He sells Heismans."

> *Tony Mason, former Arizona coach,*
> *on competing with John Robinson of*
> *USC for recruits*

"If he was 6'2", he'd be an All-American. Of course, if he was 6'2", he'd be at Southern Cal."

> *Bill Yeoman, former University of*
> *Houston coach, on 5'9" quarterback*
> *Gerald Landry*

"An American wants to play in the U.S. He's just like a sailor who is looking to get lucky every Saturday night."

> *John Bassett, owner of the Tampa Bay Bandits of the USFL, on actively recruiting American players from the Canadian Football League*

"I promised my wife twenty-seven years ago that I would take her to Florida."

> *Lee Corso, on leaving Northern Illinois to coach the Orlando Renegades of the USFL*

"I'd like to apologize to one person in particular, the man who won the 'name the team' contest and got a lifetime pass."

> *Paul Martha, president of the Pittsburgh Maulers, on the team going defunct after a year*

"It's sort of like having a friend with a serious illness and he finally passed away."

Steve Spurrier, Tampa Bay Bandits coach, on the end of the USFL

"If I can be paid what I'm paid to play in the minor leagues, I guess I'll be in the minor leagues all my life."

Herschel Walker, on signing with the USFL, which critics called football's minor league

"Now we don't have to chip in to pay the bus driver to get us to the airport."

Steve Young, on leaving the USFL for the NFL

WALK A MILE IN MY SHOES

"It shouldn't be hard to fill his shoes. He wears 12½ and I take 14."

Don Hasselbeck, on replacing Russ Francis as the Patriots' tight end

BILL WALSH

"If Bill Walsh was a general, he would be able to overrun Europe with the army from Sweden."
Beano Cook, on Bill Walsh

WAR

"When I was at North Carolina State, he bounced off our tacklers like Ethiopian spears off Mussolini's tanks."
Lou Holtz, on John Cappelletti

"I've seen better offenses than Florida State's, only they all used airplanes and tanks."
Edwin Pope, Miami
Herald *sportswriter*

WATER WORLD

"It's on the Ohio River—except every spring when it's *in* the river."

> *Lou Holtz, on his hometown of East Liverpool, Ohio*

WE ARE THE CHAMPIONS

"When you play for the national championship, it's not a matter of life or death. It's more important than that."

> *Duffy Daugherty*

WEDDED BLISS

"Because if this doesn't work out, I didn't want to blow the whole day."

> *Paul Hornung, on why he was getting married at 11 A.M.*

"I have a daughter getting married. If we don't make the playoffs, she'll have to elope."

Dick Jamieson, Cardinals running-back coach

WEIGHTY ISSUES

"Larry's so big, he was born on June 6–7–8."

Jim Carter, on 6'7" Larry Little

"He looks like someone sat down on his lap and didn't leave."

Jerry Glanville, on 300-pound Jarrell Franklin

"He can be a great player in this league for a long time if he learns to say two words—I'm full."

Jerry Glanville, on 300-pound Lincoln Kennedy

"He was eating things we couldn't even go in swimming with in Alabama."

Charley Hannah, on heavyset coach Abe Gibron

"The coaches thought he would be all-pro. He turned out to be all-cafeteria."

> *Ladd Herzog, Oilers general manager, after releasing 300-pound Angelo Fields*

"My mom goes about four bills."

> *Craig "Ironhead" Heyward, blaming his 300-pound weight on his mother*

"Does Doug Francis only weigh 260? He might have weighed that at birth. He's a house. If he had a chimney, you could sell him."

> *John McKay*

"I'm going to be in every weight-loss program available after football. I'll be into liposuction and ab-crunchers, and, if that doesn't work, then I'm going to stay in bed, eating, and having them bury me in a piano."

> *Nate Newton, 330 pounds*

"I've lost enough weight at various times to put together an entire Little League team."

> *Bubba Paris*

"It looks like a whole Dutch family moved out of the seat of them pants."

> *Bum Phillips, on 5'7", 195-pound*
> *Toni Fritsch*

"I assume he wants a team with a good chef."

> *Charley Winner, Dolphins personnel*
> *director, on 285-pound Pete Johnson*
> *naming the teams he was willing to*
> *play for*

WFL

"I've spent 11 years trying to build a serious image. I'm too far along in my career to begin playing Emmett Kelly."

> *Paul Warfield, on jumping to*
> *the WFL and wearing the*
> *league's colorful pants and*
> *different-colored jerseys*

"My wife calls me 'much maligned.' She thinks that's my first name. Every time she reads a story about me, that's always in front of my name."

Chris Bahr, placekicker

"I'd like to see Senior Miller."

Tom Brookshier, on 6'4", 235-pound Junior Miller

"They're always counting on him."

Joe Falls, on Nebraska quarterback Monte Christo

"I know why he calls everybody 'Hoss.' He can't remember anybody's name. He got in trouble. He said to my wife, 'Hey, Hoss.' That doesn't go so well."

Lou Holtz, on Cotton Bowl executive director Jim Brock

"They'll probably only use him in spots."

Alan King, on the Giants' signing of Eddie Leopard

"F.G."

James Lofton, asked his initial reaction to Forrest Gregg

"Let me know if Cain is able."

John McKay, asked if Lynn Cain of the Falcons was ready to play against the Buccaneers

"Cain't nobody spell it or pronounce it or anything."

Bum Phillips, on his given name of Oail

"As long as it's a name and not a description, it's fine with me."

O. A. "Bum" Phillips, on his nickname

"I didn't care too much for that. It's kind of embarrassing if you're a pitcher."

Dan Reeves, on playing baseball in college and having the nickname "Homerun"

"When I asked my dad about it, he told me that it had been a choice between that and Slide."

Golden Ruel, Kansas offensive
coordinator, on his name

"If it's a boy, my neighbors have some friends who want me to name him Bjorn, so the headlines could read, 'Bjorn Zorn born.'"

Jim Zorn, on possible names for
his child

WIDE RECEIVERS

"We'd like our receivers to have both, but if they had both, they'd be at USC."

LaVell Edwards, BYU coach, on what
was more important for receivers—
speed or quickness

"He's like a diner—he's open all the time."

Jimmy the Greek, on Roy Green

"If they did, I'd stomp 'em and do a pirouette on their head."

Ken Avery, retired Bengals linebacker, on what he would do if people called him a sissy for learning ballet

"Red is kind of a wimpy color. Maybe next year they'll make us wear little flowers on our jerseys, up around the shoulder pads. And then they could have Big Bird on the side of our pants to make the kids happy."

Fred Smerlas, on the Bills changing from white to red helmets

"Anytime you have a situation where you score, then they score, and it goes back and forth—that's no fun. It was a test, a matchup. Checkers with your daughter is fun. This wasn't."

> *Dave Casper, on an AFC divisional*
> *playoff game won by the Raiders*
> *over the Colts, 37–31*

"It's better to go 7–3 than 9–1. When you go 7–3, everybody talks about the games you won. When you go 9–1, all anybody talks about is the game you lost."

> *Doug Dickey, former University of*
> *Florida football coach*

"As the famous artist Vincent van Gogh would say, 'Gang, it wasn't a masterpiece, but it will sell.'"

> *Mike Ditka, after the Bears beat the*
> *Packers, 12–10*

"There comes a time when you have enough deceased presidents and you play for the ring."

> *Lester Hayes, on a championship*
> *meaning more than money*

"Without winners, there wouldn't be any civilization."

Woody Hayes

"You never get ahead of anyone as long as you try to get even with him."

Lou Holtz

"There isn't anything wrong with winning ugly. As a matter of fact, there isn't anything wrong with being ugly—as long as you're successful."

Lou Holtz

"Winning is like shaving—you have to do it every day or you wind up looking like a bum."

Jack Kemp

"When you're not a winner, you have to stand in line for picture shows; but when you're a winner, you go in the back door with the manager."

Bobby Layne

"Beat your opponent where he is strongest, and you demoralize him."

Vince Lombardi

"Winning isn't everything, but wanting to win is."
Vince Lombardi

"If you can accept losing, you can't win. If you can walk, you can run. No one is ever hurt. Hurt is in your mind."
Vince Lombardi

"If I ever get so greedy that I'm not satisfied to win by one point, than I'll know there's something wrong with me."
Ben Schwartzwalder, former
Syracuse coach

"Life is better than death only when you're winning."
Ben Schwartzwalder

"We decided . . . we were going to eat Rice. Why not, 70 percent of the world does."
Darren Yancey, BYU linebacker, after
beating Rice, 49–0

WISE MAN

"Some coaches pray for wisdom. I pray for 260-pound tackles. They'll give me plenty of wisdom."
Chuck Mills

WOLVERINES

"This year we've got Michigan just where we want them. We don't play them."
Lee Corso, former Indiana coach

WORK OF ART

"You've got a better chance of completing a pass to the Venus de Milo."
Vance Johnson, on Quadry Ismail

"Well, we do have a draw play."
Pat McInally, on how his art classes at Harvard helped him in the NFL

WORKING STIFF

"You've got to like any job where you don't have to go to work until noon."

John Riggins

STEVE YOUNG

"I'm not scared. He's the one running it."

Leeman Bennett, Buccaneers coach, asked if he was scared when Buccaneers quarterback Steve Young was running with the ball

YOUTH

"People talk about having an inferiority complex. Me, I did have a complex—I *was* inferior."

Lou Holtz, on his youth

INDEX

263